DRAWING UNDER FIRE

War Diary of a Young Vietnamese Artist

Phạm Thanh Tâm

ASIA INK, London

Reviews

Vietnamese-Language Edition, 2024

"This is a special book, worth noting among the publications released for the Seventieth Anniversary of the Victory of Điện Biên Phủ. At the age of twenty-two, Phạm Thanh Tâm joined the Điện Biên Phủ Campaign as a war correspondent and artist. In his first diary entry, he wrote: 'I went to the campaign with half of the art troupe. Happy and enthusiastic because I felt healthy, although a bit thin.'

In addition to the diary content, the more than thirty sketches drawn by the author in the trenches have special value.

According to artist Lương Xuân Đoàn, Chairman of the Vietnam Fine Arts Association: 'Phạm Thanh Tâm's sketches are full of emotion. The artist draws the delicate feelings of soldiers parting from their lovers, caring for wounded comrades, enjoying a stream after a fierce fight on Hill E, and the joy of peace when flowers bloom on broken helmets.'"

Giáng Ngọc, "A Special Sketchbook by Artist Phạm Thanh Tâm," *The People's Army Online Newspaper,* May 15, 2024

"A valuable historical document and a unique emotional expression of the Điện Biên Phủ Campaign. At the age of twenty-two, the young Phạm Thanh Tâm joined the Điện Biên Phủ Campaign as a war correspondent

The war reporter and artist Phạm Thanh Tâm
(1932–2019) at Điện Biên Phủ in 2007.
The Witness Collection Archive.

and artist. The diary was written directly on the battlefield, right in the trenches, under bombs and bullets. His notes during these days are vivid and vital documents ... His sketches equally vivid and emotional, as he lived with the soldiers during the most difficult days of the Battle of Điện Biên Phủ."

"Book Launch and Online Exhibition of the Điện Biên Phủ Battlefield Diary by Artist Phạm Thanh Tâm," *VIETNAM.VN,* May 6, 2024

"Tâm's diary and sketches is the most notable publication of the Seventieth Anniversary of the Battle of Điện Biên Phủ ... Tâm's sketches are full of emotion."

Hà Trang, "Sketches in the Trenches: Memories of a Reporter at the Điện Biên Phủ Campaign," *Education and Times Online Newspaper,* May 7, 2024

French-Language Edition, 2011

"In February 1954, the twenty-two-year-old Phạm Thanh Tâm, painfully thin after seven years of conflict but still full of enthusiasm, leaves for Điện Biên Phủ, wearing his sandals and rice belt. Armed only with pencils and brushes, the student of the Hanoi Fine Arts Institute, trained in French classical drawing, is attached to the Việt Minh artillery division.

He keeps a diary and draws in pencil, ink, and watercolor what he sees during and after the battles: landscapes burnt by napalm and aerial bombings, comrades-in-arms, wounded and frightened or buoyed by the sayings of Uncle Hồ, fire and death.

If this illustrated diary is not without its ideological clarion calls, it is one of the rare ... Việt Minh diaries of this battle. All the more credit to the American journalist Sherry Buchanan for having found and meticulously edited this account that ends in August 1954, when Tâm returns to Hanoi. "Every fall I have the feeling that we will go to war," he writes.

Ten years later, he is called upon to draw the first American plane shot down over North Vietnam."

Emmanuel Hecht, "The Last French Battle Seen from the Việt Minh Side: An Extraordinary Testimony," *L'Express,* March 14, 2011

"There is an extensive bibliography of the Battle of Điện Biên Phủ, the epic event that in May 1954 signaled the death knell of French Indochina. However the rarity of Việt Minh contemporaneous accounts of this momentous battle makes this recently discovered diary of a twenty-two-year-old soldier all the more precious.

Phạm Thanh Tâm was a student at the Hanoi Fine Arts Institute when he enlisted with the artillery division as a war reporter. With his *maquisards* comrades, he sets off on a five-hundred-kilometer trek through the punishing Tonkin jungle to Điện Biên Phủ where General Navarre, commander of the French Far East Expeditionary Corps, had built a French military base deemed to be impregnable.

To secure the base, the 'red ants' of the Vietnam People's Army pulled their two-ton cannons on marches that lasted up to twenty hours a day, dug trenches, and built underground casemates. The battle raged for fifty-five days until the surrender of the French commander General de Castries on May 7 ...

Tâm's precious diary is crammed with detail. As a revolutionary scribe, above all he records the courage of his comrades. Yet going beyond military censorship, he also expresses their sadness and suffering.

The artist is ever present, showcasing his text with drawings and watercolors. Portraits of soldiers, artillerymen in action, and dark landscapes of war are contrasted with bucolic scenes that he sketches elegantly between steel deluges of air power."
"Diaries from Indochina," *Le Figaro*, May 12, 2011

"May 7, 1954, in the valley of Điện Biên Phủ, was a traumatic event for the French Army. In the ranks of the Việt Minh, Phạm Thanh Tâm, a twenty-two-year-old war reporter, kept a diary of the battle. In this extremely rare diary, the propaganda does not alter the underlying emotions." *Le Nouvel Observateur*, March 2011

"In this poignant and elegant book, Phạm Thanh Tâm records the events of the Battle of Điện Biên Phủ from the Việt Minh soldiers' perspective. Hundreds if not thousands of books have been written on the Indochina War, the first great conflict of French decolonization, that lasted from 1946 to July 27, 1954. The French defeat at Điện Biên Phủ on May 7,

1954 remains one of the most traumatic events in French military history. The majority of the accounts of the battle are by French veterans shocked at their defeat against a Việt Minh adversary who fought for their homeland under the communist banner.

Only a few rare accounts by the victorious enemy exist. This is why Phạm Thanh Tâm's diary is of such significance. When Phạm Thanh Tâm begins his diary, although only twenty-two, he has already spent seven years at war. A former student of the Việt Bắc Fine Arts College, he is named war correspondent for the artillery division (F351) of the Vietnam People's Army.

He leaves for the front with some blank notebooks, a pen, and a Waterman ink bottle as his weapons. The French forces believed the military base at Điện Biên Phủ to be impregnable being too difficult for the Việt Minh heavy artillery to reach.

As the American journalist Sherry Buchanan points out:

'In order to make their way to Điện Biên Phủ, the People's Army's engineers would have to purpose-build hundreds of kilometers of roads to make way for their heavy artillery. A feat believed to be impossible by the American advisors and the French generals. Yet, against all expectations, the Việt Minh built the roads.'

Phạm Thanh Tâm chronicles the historic march towards Điện Biên Phủ. The two-ton 105mm cannons that would smash the French garrison were pulled and hoisted up vertiginous hills, inch by inch, amidst a thousand perils. As for the dismountable cannon parts, the soldiers carried them through the steep jungle terrain on their backs.

The diary is illustrated with beautiful and elegant sketches and watercolors. This is a must-read, for the strength of the account told without hatred." Jean Guisnel, 'The French Defeat at Điện Biên Phủ Seen from the Việt Minh Side," *Le Point*, 2011

"On May 7, 1954 … the French forces at Điện Biên Phủ surrendered to the Vietnam People's Army. Much has been written on this subject, yet the Việt Minh accounts of the battle are extremely rare and we know little of how the conflict was viewed from the perspective of the soldiers fighting on the Vietnamese communist side.

This diary, discovered by the American journalist Sherry Buchanan, is an instructive response. The author, a twenty-two-year-old student of the Hanoi Fine Arts Institute, was a war reporter with the Vietnam People's Army. In his diary, he records the battle and the thoughts of his fellow soldiers.

Although written in the propaganda style of the day, the underlying emotions reveal the universality of suffering in war. Along with an introduction by Sherry Buchanan, this exceptional diary offers a new perspective on the French Indochina War." *Le Club Histoire*, 2011

UK Edition, 2005

"Phạm Thanh Tâm's *Drawing Under Fire* is an amazing book. Tâm was fifteen when he joined the Resistance against the French after his home was destroyed in the 1946 French bombing of the city. Living under cover, he sketched and reported what he saw.

In 1954 he covered the historic Battle of Điện Biên Phủ. Later, during the Vietnam War, he was an official artist throughout the Tết Offensive. His is an incredible story; his illustrations and reportage are equally memorable."

Tim Teeman, INTERALIA Book Review, *The Times*, June 11, 2005

"*Drawing Under Fire* is the Vietnamese equivalent of Graham Greene's *The Quiet American*. A unique wartime diary, more exciting than fiction with extraordinary drawings and sketches done during the Battle of Điện Biên Phủ."

Philip Dodd, *Night Waves*, **BBC Radio 3**, May 11, 2005

"A poignant and timely insight into the North Vietnamese side of the conflict." **BBC Radio Humberside**, June 2, 2005

"A unique and thoroughly fascinating diary of words, drawings, and painting." **BBC Radio Jersey**, June 7, 2005

"An innovative and beautifully presented book." **BBC Radio Wiltshire**, June 13, 2005

"This is an extraordinary secret history by Vietnam's lost war artist. In 1954, Phạm Thanh Tâm kept a diary of life on the front in the war for independence. It was then hidden away until a chance meeting fifty years later."

Sherry Buchanan, "Vietnam's Lost War Artist," *The Independent*, May 25, 2005

"*Drawing Under Fire* [is] a beautifully produced edition of a war diary by a young artist, Phạm Thanh Tâm, written and sketched during the epic Battle of Điện Biên Phủ (1954). In this poetic document, discovered by Asia Ink's founder and publisher Sherry Buchanan, a young man seeks to share his dreams of beauty and love with his fellow-soldiers."

Vivienne Menkes, *Publishing News*, November 19, 2005

"Artists also boosted the morale of combat soldiers ... as the artist Phạm Thanh Tâm told Sherry Buchanan: 'Soldiers enjoyed having me around drawing. They thought it was relaxing. To have someone remembering you by drawing you—it was like telling a beautiful girl she was beautiful.'"

Alan Riding, "The Vietnam War as Seen in Art from the Other Side," *The New York Times,* November 22, 2002

"Phạm Thanh Tâm learned the *croquis rapide* (quick sketching technique) in the Việt Bắc, Hồ Chí Minh's remote jungle headquarters during the Indochina War. His teachers were some of the most talented artists of their generation. Inheritors of the French neo-classical style introduced to Vietnam in 1925, they followed Hồ Chí Minh into the jungle and set up an art school in the Resistance Zone to teach 'art for the people.' Some of the results can be seen in the exhibition *Vietnam Behind the Lines*, which opens at the British Museum this week."

Sherry Buchanan, "Drawing Fire," *The Guardian*, June 10, 2002

Readers' Comments

"This diary is wonderful. The author should be elected living treasure for humanity. It's a great read, and very poignant at times. I understand why they 'won' every time, and would win again if it happened again. What an extraordinary young man the author was!" **Marie-Caroline van Herpen**, Paris

"A remarkable book." **Pierre d'Anchalt**, Điện Biên Phủ veteran

"I loved Phạm Thanh Tâm's diary. Boy, why didn't we read this before going into Vietnam?" **Douglas Young**, Korean War veteran

"An exciting book. The serenity of the drawings amidst the horror is remarkable. Such calm in the storm!" **Reynier Pozzo di Borgo**, Paris

DRAWING UNDER FIRE

War Diary of a Young Vietnamese Artist

Phạm Thanh Tâm

Preface by Jessica Harrison-Hall
Translated by Nguyễn Vân Hà
Edited by Sherry Buchanan

Điện Biên

KM 70 ☐

CH Sở??

Km 69

15 km — Bác Nam qua đường Pha Sông

BCH Cz Trần Đình   Đợt I / cg
                     vào ... ra
14/1 - 54

BCH Chuẩn ... Mường Phăng

vấn đề lớn !
2 cách đánh
BCH Cz bãi chợ bể 357

Navarre, o Danies Va Castrie

Published by Asia Ink
1 Alma Terrace
London W8 6QY, United Kingdom
www.asiainkbooks.com
sbuchanan@asiainkbooks.com

Distributed by The University of Chicago Press

First published by Asia Ink 2005
First published in paperback by Asia Ink 2024

Translator: Nguyễn Vân Hà
Designer: Misha Anikst
Photographer: Hans Kemp
Proofreader: Helen Cumberbatch

A catalogue record for this book is available from the British Library.

ISBN 978-1-9163463-6-9 (paperback)
ISBN 978-0-9537839-3-9 (cloth)

Title page: Facsimile of Tâm's hand-drawn map of the road to
Điện Biên Phủ, 1954, 22 x 28cm. Collection of the Điện Biên Phủ
Museum. The page features the name of John W. O'Daniel, the
chief of the US Military Assistance Advisory Group for Indochina
(MAAG) and advisor to the French commanders at Điện Biên Phủ.
The United States, although not an official party to the war, gave
full military and financial support to the French forces.

Contents

14 Preface
    Jessica Harrison-Hall
20 The Artist Under Fire
    Sherry Buchanan
46 The Artist on the Battlefield

50 On the Road
80 In the Trenches
162 Going Home

186 Map and Timeline
190 Notes
209 Select Bibliography
214 Editor's Acknowledgements

là ...
... uỷ trị tình ...
My traliên cho __C 8 03 ...
... to uyế t thiế bàng ngồi trên
vai 1 bát dầu ... báo cáo ngay
từ lúc 4 giờ 12 bắt
16 lượng
16 giờ 25
9 (.) từ lạc ...
Đông Nam sân bay
801 1 bát trung
Loạt 3 chung
— 802 2 loạt đạn
— 62 (3) loạt đạn
— trúng ... tiêu !
đạn
... tiếp ... Faobin trú
... bắn vai F
03 bắn vai F
... bay
... bay hanôn
Ktru 2 bà già
... ở Mười Trang
trên
... truy trên Fao dịch 203

Preface
Jessica Harrison-Hall

Journalist and artist Phạm Thanh Tâm (1932–2019) wrote his extra-ordinary diary during the Battle of Điện Biên Phủ in 1954. The Việt Minh (*Việt Nam Độc lập Đồng minh*) victory against the French colonial power marked the end of French colonial rule in Indochina, secured Vietnamese independence, and led to the American Vietnam War (1964–1975). This new edition of Phạm Thanh Tâm's original manuscript and sketches, published to commemorate the seventieth anniversary of the battle, reveals the accuracy of Tâm's account checked against newly available North Vietnamese sources. The manuscript is in the collection of the Điện Biên Phủ Museum.

The diary is a rare eyewitness account written under fire during the historic battle. It is beautifully illustrated with sketches drawn on the battlefield. Few original sketches created during the French War (1946–1954) survive, and even fewer have been catalogued and published.

The British Museum is privileged to have drawings by Phạm Thanh Tâm in its permanent collection of Vietnamese war art.

Opposite: Author's ink bottle and pen, and facsimile of the diary page dated March 13, 1954, the first attack by the People's Army against the French fortress, 22 x 14cm. Collection of the Điện Biên Phủ Museum.

The Diary

Phạm Thanh Tâm wrote his diary in minute script. The diary remained hidden until 2002, when the journalist and historian Sherry Buchanan discovered it while researching art created during the American Vietnam War for the publication *Mekong Diaries: Artists' Stories & Drawings 1964–1975* (University of Chicago Press, 2008).

The diary was first published to critical acclaim in the United Kingdom in 2005 by Asia Ink, in France in 2011 by Armand Colin, and in 2014 by Kim Đồng Publishing House (see Reviews).

The twenty-two-year-old artist wrote the diary when he was a war correspondent with *Determined to Win* (*Quyết chiến, Quyết thắng*), the newspaper published by the heavy artillery division of the People's Army. Before enlisting in the Army, he had completed his art studies at the Việt Bắc College of Art in the Resistance Zone. His teachers—notably Bùi Xuân Phái—were graduates of the prestigious École des Beaux-Arts d'Indochine, created in 1925 by the French.

The diary starts on February 26, 1954, as Phạm Thanh Tâm sets off from Yên Bái to cross the Red River with the heavy artillery division of Vietnam's People's Army, marching to the front to lay siege to the French military fortress in the remote valley of Điện Biên Phủ.

Writing under fire, he shares his emotions and chronicles the historic battle over fifty-five days and nights, between March 13 and May 7, 1954. The diary ends on August 28, 1954, when Phạm Thanh Tâm returns to Hanoi at the end of the First Indochina War (1946–1954).

His watercolors based on battlefield sketches won third prize at the National Fine Arts Exhibition held in Hanoi to celebrate the Việt Minh victory at Điện Biên Phủ.

Phạm Thanh Tâm carried his pen, pencils, and Chinese ink bottle into battle, sketching portraits of soldiers, Youth Volunteers, and Thái villagers, cannons, and *Molotova* trucks, and maps of the battlefield.

This important historical document provides rare insights from participants fighting on the Việt Minh side against the colonial forces. Tâm records the soldiers' emotions, their courage, their resilience, and their suffering.

Hundreds of books by Vietnamese, French, American, and English authors have been published chronicling the war—notably by General

*"I wrote and sketched in the style of the time,
a socialist-realist style,
and I wrote with all my heart."*

Phạm Thanh Tâm

Võ Nguyên Giáp, the commander of the People's Army, and strategist of Vietnam's victories against the French and the Americans—but few are contemporaneous eyewitness accounts.

Phạm Thanh Tâm recounts the extraordinary odyssey of artillerymen and foot soldiers who dragged two-ton cannons across the rugged mountain terrain of the north of Vietnam. Under relentless bombing raids, they dug shelters to camouflage the cannons, and besieged the French fortress of Điện Biên Phủ, which was thought to be impregnable. As a military reporter, Tâm benefited from his unique access to artillerymen, political commissars, and senior officers. The heavy artillery division of the People's Army was crucial to Võ Nguyên Giáp's strategy to win against the superior French colonial forces.

Tâm's battlefield notes, soldiers' accounts, and personal observations have a rawness and poignancy that come from the immediacy of his reports. Although not a combatant himself, he was one of them. He was close in age to the eighteen-year-old soldiers, he didn't carry a gun, and trusted his armed comrades with his life.

In the tradition of war reporters and artists of World War I and the Spanish Civil War, Tâm moved around the battlefield, through the muddy, bloody trenches, to collect firsthand accounts of the battles. He slept next to the cannons in underground shelters, he joined tunnel-digging teams, and marched with the troops hauling cannons. He composed revolutionary songs and poems, reading them aloud before the attacks to encourage his friends into battle. He sketched portraits of the soldiers and organized recreational activities—sharing a cigarette was rated as a social event, to "keep up morale and calm the mind."

Drawings and Sketches
It is inspiring that Phạm Thanh Tâm found the peace of mind to sketch and write. Điện Biên Phủ is remembered as a sanguinary battle. American journalist Bernard B. Fall famously described the battlefield as "hell in a very small place." Fighters confronted each other in hand-to-hand combat in the trenches and on the bare hilltops under relentless bombing attacks.

The quiet poetry of Tâm's drawings and sketches express the loneliness of a young artist in war, sharing his dreams of love, friendship, and beauty with his fellow soldiers.

He created lyrical portraits of wistful women fighters and civilians. He drew pensive combatants. He recorded intimate scenes of soldiers at rest, writing letters home, sharing thoughts, smoking strong tobacco in water pipes, and playing cards. The inscriptions on the back of the drawings and sketches that describe the activities he was depicting have been included in the captions.

The power of his works comes from the artist's intent to convey meaning through his drawings.

As he explained in a conversation with Sherry Buchanan:

"Bùi Xuân Phái used to tell us to keep the composition simple, that one detail is enough to express meaning. A painting should be elegant but meaningful. I never forgot his advice."

Phạm Thanh Tâm used pen and ink, pencil, black crayon, and chalk. Some are finished drawings, others are sketches.

After the war, he painted larger-scale watercolors based on his battlefront sketches. His watercolors were exhibited at the 1954 National Fine Arts Exhibition that was held in Hanoi to celebrate the Điện Biên Phủ victory, where he was awarded third prize.

Phạm Thanh Tâm's drawings and sketches are a universal tribute to all the young men and women, combatants and civilians, who perish in war.

Jessica Harrison-Hall
Head of the China section
The British Museum, London
March 31, 2024

The Artist Under Fire
Sherry Buchanan

"War is always terrible."
Phạm Thanh Tâm greeted me with a strong handshake, the straight back
of a military man, and an open smile. The war artist had invited me to
look at his collection of war drawings at his house in Ho Chi Minh City.

I was in Vietnam to do a story for the *International Herald Tribune* on
the drawings created on the front line by former enemy artists during
the American Vietnam War (1964–1975).

Why, you might ask, was I interested in showing the other side of the
Vietnam War? Art created in war represents the triumph of humanity
over the dehumanization and destruction of war. The images offered
glimpses of redemption to the cruel conflict I had watched unfold on
the nightly CBS News in my college dorm at Smith College.

That evening, in 2002, his effervescent wife Lê Thị Lân cooked a
sumptuous meal of fried spring rolls, giant snails, and northern sweets.

After dinner, Tâm toasted to our meeting with a homemade brew.

"*Một! Hai! Ba! Dzô!*" he said, raising his glass.

"Delicious," I replied, choking on the firewater.

He fetched his war memorabilia, medals, a military uniform,
and art tools.

Opposite: Canteen used by the author during
the Battle of Điện Biên Phủ. Collection of the
Ho Chi Minh City Fine Arts Museum.

"My Waterman pen, paintbrushes, a palette knife, and the 12.7mm empty case of a Soviet shell," he said.

"What was the bullet for?" I asked.

"I used it as an inkwell!" he answered, proud of his invention.

"I've been trying to get him to get rid of all these old things for years," Lân said. She smiled, knowing he never would.

Tâm saved the iron helmet for last. The rusty metal was full of holes.

"These aren't bullet holes! I used the helmet as a watering can after the war!" he explained, laughing at the idea.

He then dragged an iron chest out from under a bed in the living room. There were stacks of drawings inside. Tâm had preserved hundreds of sketches, Chinese ink drawings, watercolors on paper, and small oils on board. A collection of this size was rare. Artists had lost their drawings to bombs, floods, termites, and the passage of time.

Tâm began leafing through the works. Every drawing brought back a memory, a story: a Hanoi street destroyed by US bombs in 1965, the portrait of a young woman with an AK47 on the Ho Chi Minh Trail, soldiers crossing a river on the way to Khe Sanh, the 1968 Tết Offensive, and a victorious tank entering Saigon in 1975.

"These are my true memories. They are my soul," he said.

That first evening with Mr Tâm and Mrs Lân led to many more. The house offered warmth and hospitality, a place to talk and exchange ideas, to look at drawings and remember the past, where friendship bridged wars.

One evening, on my way back to my apartment in the center of town after an evening session chez Tâm and Lân, I was surprised to find that the alley outside their house had turned into a fast-flowing river. The monsoon rains had started.

"Too dangerous to drive. Let's wait until the water level comes down," said Tâm.

We looked at more drawings. Lân sat beside us, fully engaged, while Tâm talked and I took notes, recording the stories that accompanied each drawing. A pencil sketch of a soldier caught my eye. The fighter was aiming a bayonet used in the First Indochina War (1946–1954).

I checked the date: 1954 was the last year of Vietnam's war of independence from French colonial rule.

"Were you in the war against the French?" I asked, surprised.

"Yes," he answered.

Tâm didn't look old enough. The artist had the energy and gait of a much younger man.

I pushed my luck.

"Were you at the Battle of Điện Biên Phủ?" I inquired.

Điện Biên Phủ was a historically significant battle in the annals of colonialism: the Việt Minh victory marked the end of French colonial rule in Indochina. But the 1954 Geneva Accords provisionally partitioned the colonial territory into communist North and anti-communist South Vietnam, pending national elections for reunification by 1956. The elections never happened, opposed by South Vietnam and the United States. This led directly to the American Vietnam War (1964–1975).

"Yes, I sketched a lot during the battle."

"Do you have any left?"

"Of course."

"Did you keep a diary?" I ventured.

He didn't answer. He stuck his cigarette between his lips, thought for a moment, and disappeared upstairs.

I waited. Lân served up more spring rolls. I wasn't sure what to expect.

Tâm returned carrying an old cardboard box. Two inches of moist, black, moldy dust clung to the lid.

I wondered if the contents had survived.

Tâm opened the box full of paper documents that had been wrapped in plastic to protect them from the termites that eat away at Vietnam's paper heritage.

He took out a notebook covered in cloth; a faded blue, once brilliant.

"I had forgotten about the diary, until now when you asked. I wrote it during the fifty-five days of the Điện Biên Phủ Campaign in 1954," Tâm said.

I had read hundreds of accounts of the battle by French, American, and Vietnamese veterans, historians, and journalists. Few, if any, were written during the battle.

Fifty years on, I had stumbled upon a rare contemporaneous account of the historic battle from an anti-colonial perspective.

Facsimile of pages from Tâm's diary, 1954,
22 x 28cm. Collection of the Điện Biên Phủ
Museum. Photographs from left to right: Tâm and
friends at the entrance to an underground bunker;
portraits of Tâm in Army uniform; and posing with
Thái villagers in front of a French tank captured
at Điện Biên Phủ. Collection of the artist.

"We should publish this," I said.

"*Một! Hai! Ba! Dzô!*" Tâm said, raising his glass of firewater.

I took the toast as a yes!

It was past midnight. I perched on the back of a moped for the ride home. Tâm's neighbor drove me back through the silent streets to my place in the center of town.

I returned to Vietnam two years later to transcribe, translate, and photograph Phạm Thanh Tâm's diary for publication.

Over the next month, we met every day. This introduction is drawn from the daily interviews I conducted in 2004 at his house in Ho Chi Minh City, and from subsequent meetings until 2015.

We talked about his childhood in Haiphong, his adolescence in the Resistance, his time at art college, and his years as a journalist with front-line newspapers. I discovered that the emotions and beliefs expressed in his diary and sketches were deeply rooted in a childhood and adolescence marked by colonialism and traumatic historical events: the rise of Vietnamese nationalism and resistance to French colonial rule, the Japanese occupation of Vietnam (1940–1945) during World War II, the human-made famine by the occupiers, the proclamation of Vietnamese independence at the end of the war on September 2, 1945, the reoccupation of Vietnam by the French colonial power, and the First Indochina War (1946–1954).

Childhood Memories, 1932–1946: "My sketches are my soul."

Tâm was born in the northern port city of Haiphong during Vietnamese resistance to French colonial rule. He grew up in a revolutionary family. His parents, who worked for *La Cimenterie*, the French-owned cement factory and the city's main employer, supported Vietnamese independence.

When Tâm was ten, his parents joined the League for the Liberation of Vietnam (*Việt Nam Độc lập Đồng minh*). The Việt Minh, created by Hồ Chí Minh in 1941, united communist and non-communist nationalists in their fight for independence.

Marxist–Leninism, as Tâm points out in his diary, was the ideology of necessity for nationalists in oppressed colonial territories seeking independence and sovereignty. Hồ Chí Minh had hoped for US support, and wrote to US presidents Woodrow Wilson and Franklin D. Roosevelt, but his requests for

US backing against French colonial rule were ignored.

Tâm remembers a happy enough childhood, caught between the shadow of French oppression and the promise of a free Vietnam. The contradictions of colonialism were not lost on the young schoolboy. Tâm attended the French lycée, named after the trader Jean Dupuis who assisted in the conquest of Vietnam.

"Our history class used to start with: *Nos ancêtres les Gaulois*—our ancestors, the Gauls," he remembers, smiling at the quirkiness of colonial history classes.

He was equally perplexed by the uncivilized behavior of those who claimed to bring "civilization" to the Vietnamese.

"French soldiers used to urinate on our heads from a bridge in town. Why did they do that?" he asked, shaking his head, looking for an answer.

The most shocking experience of his adolescence was witnessing the human-made famine of 1944–1945 (*Nạn đói năm Ất Dậu*) and the inhumanity of the engineered starvation that killed between four hundred thousand and two million people. The Japanese occupation forces requisitioned rice for export to Japan, while the Vichy French administrators stored rice for their own use, leaving the farmers to starve.

Tâm grimaced as he remembered the horrors he saw:

"Farmers came into Haiphong looking for food. They were skeletal. They were covered in open sores, crawling with maggots. They died in the street. It was a terrible way to die. We buried the bodies in mass graves. Those who survived the famine joined the Resistance," he said.

The First Indochina War, 1946–1954: "Down with War."

Tâm's adolescence was cut short by the outbreak of war. With a global sense of peace after two world wars, Vietnam became engulfed in three decades of war.

When Tâm was fourteen, Hồ Chí Minh proclaimed Vietnamese independence on September 2, 1945, quoting from the American Declaration of Independence. But Vietnamese independence was short-lived. The French returned to reclaim their colony. The reoccupation by the Far East Expeditionary Corps in Indochina led to the First Indochina War.

Hồ Chí Minh and his government evacuated Hanoi to set up head-quarters in the Resistance Zone or Việt Bắc, the rugged mountainous region northeast of Hanoi. Nationalists and communists loyal to Hồ Chí Minh followed, swelling the ranks of the Việt Minh to an estimated five hundred thousand members.

Tâm and his family left their home in Haiphong for the Resistance at the end of December 1946, after the French Navy bombarded the city's harbor, killing an estimated six thousand civilians.

"I joined the Resistance when I had just turned fifteen," he said.

"Did you call it the Resistance?" I asked.

"Yes. We named it after the French Resistance against the Nazis who occupied France during World War II," he explained.

Tâm's father secured a job in the government's arts and propaganda department. Tâm volunteered to courier articles penned by Resistance writers and poets to newspapers in French-occupied Hanoi.

The artist Mai Văn Nam, who worked with his father, noticed young Tâm had a natural talent for drawing, and encouraged him to apply to the Việt Bắc College of Art, set up by professors of the École des Beaux-Arts d'Indochine who had fled occupied Hanoi.

Tâm was accepted into the first class of the new art school. Artists

Lương Xuân Nhị (1913–2006) and Bùi Xuân Phái (1920–1988), painting masters of twentieth-century Vietnamese painting, were his teachers.

He channeled his adolescent quest for romance into a love of art and country. The first-year art course *Down with War* trained Resistance artists and fighters in French classical-art techniques.

In his new surroundings, the city boy from Haiphong was inspired to sketch the beauty of the countryside that was now his home.

"Phái used to tell us to keep the composition simple, that one detail is enough to express meaning. A painting should be elegant but meaningful. I never forgot his advice," he remembered.

At the same time, he was proficient in the propaganda art used to mobilize the rural population, a key part of the Việt Minh's war strategy against the French.

Tâm's first job after art school was as a wartime Banksy. It was dangerous work. He was dispatched by the propaganda department to villages in the French-occupied zone. The area was patrolled by French security units tracking down Việt Minh fighters and sympathizers.

Tâm painted revolutionary slogans and images on the walls of public buildings and houses. Separated from his parents, he found shelter and food with families who supported the Resistance. He operated alone.

Demonstrators hold a protest rally in Hanoi in 1946 in support of Hồ Chí Minh, leader of the independence movement. The banners are similar to those Tâm designed in the Resistance. An inscription reads: "We support our leader Uncle Hồ (*Ủng hộ Hộ chú lịch*)."

He moved from place to place to evade the deadly French Army patrols:

"I found a wall, drew quickly, usually at night, and then ran for my life. I was afraid but, given the situation, I had to do it. I wasn't a soldier, so I didn't have a gun to defend myself. If you were caught, you were killed. I lost a lot of friends that way. Many disappeared. I never saw them again. I was too young to know what death really meant."

"Did you have time to draw?" I asked.

"Yes, once, when there was less fighting," he said.

He remembers an idyllic occasion when he stayed for a week in a village in a peaceful rural setting.

"It was a wonderful time because I loved painting. I was so young, only seventeen, and I lived in harmony with nature and art."

He added:

"I missed my family, but it was the same for all of us. The youngest in our group was only ten years old—it was normal to be away from your family at the time."

Reporting the Resistance, 1950–1954: "Sure to Win."

The war escalated. Tâm's propaganda work in the French-occupied zone became increasingly risky. The United States feared the expansion of communism in Southeast Asia after Mao Zedong's victory in the People's Republic of China in 1949. Under the Truman Doctrine, the United States provided political, military, and economic assistance to the French colonial forces fighting against communism.

The emboldened French occupying forces launched a counterinsurgency to eradicate the Resistance fighters.

Tâm remembered the terror the French unleashed in the countryside:

"The French arrested all the young men in the village, even those who weren't caught doing anything subversive. If you were caught, you were killed. The French didn't release anybody alive.

"When they raided villages they divided people into two groups.

Opposite: *Portrait of a Thái child*, Điện Biên Phủ, 1954, graphite on paper, 18 x 12cm. Collection of the artist.

Young men on one side; women, children, and older people on the other. They shot all the young men. Of the women, children, and older people, they only shot those they suspected of being Việt Minh."

"What did you do?" I asked.

"I wasn't armed and the situation was becoming extremely dangerous. So I joined the Army," he explained.

The Việt Minh's forces were renamed the Việt Nam People's Army in 1950. In May of that year, Tâm enlisted and got a job with *Sure to Win* (*Tất Thắng*), the newspaper of the E34 regiment, headquartered in Nam Định. The paper had one reporter and six printers.

Between 1950 and 1953, the enterprising Tâm worked as an illustrator and reporter. He covered the regiment's military operations and wrote stories about resistance to French occupation.

He explained:

"When I was an artist in the villages, I couldn't have survived without the help of the people. They didn't have much themselves, but they fed and housed me. It was very dangerous for the families I lived with. If they were caught they were killed. As a journalist, these were the stories I wrote about."

The People's Army became his new family.

"Once I joined the Army, I no longer worked alone in the villages. My new friends were armed. I could rely on them to protect me," he said.

Tâm remembers the privations of Army life, but also the friendships that sustained him during these difficult times, a recurring theme in the diary:

"Everything was rationed. Food, clothes, blankets. I slept on the ground. I wrapped myself in straw against the cold. I had a shirt, a pair of trousers, a bamboo hat, and bare feet. I was too poor to buy sandals!

"I was always getting sick when I was on my own. I was too young to know how to take care of myself.

"A few months after I joined the Army, I got malaria. Two of my friends from the regiment cared for me. We didn't have a doctor and the clinic was far away. They gave me limes to cure the malaria and rice wine to cure my stomach!

"I was lucky! One guy with malaria had to swallow a huge worm! Live! But it worked and he was cured!

"We had one bowl of rice a day. But my friends made sure I got two. They also gave me extra peanuts and vegetables. The peanuts were as gritty as gunpowder and the vegetables as prickly as barbed wire!"

Điện Biên Phủ, 1954: "Determined to Win."

The French by 1953 were losing ground to the Việt Minh who had gained widespread popular support after the famine, and following their promise to introduce a land reform and literacy program.

In May 1953, French Premier René Mayer appointed Henri Navarre to take command of the French Far East Expeditionary Corps in Indochina. Navarre built an "impregnable fortress" defended by air power, tanks, and heavy artillery to protect French-controlled territory against Việt Minh incursions until an "honorable political solution" could be found.

The Politburo and General Võ Nguyên Giáp, the commander of the People's Army, decided to attack and besiege the French military fortress located in a remote valley on the border with Laos.

Tâm's regiment became part of Artillery Division 351 that would prove decisive in the Battle of Điện Biên Phủ. He joined the staff of the division's newspaper, *Determined to Win* (*Quyết chiến, Quyết thắng*), excited to be a correspondent with an important unit of the People's Army. He was sent for military training to a camp near Kunming, in Yunnan, in southwest China. As odd as it may sound now and as hard as the training was, he enjoyed his time there.

"Away from the war, I found time to sketch," he explained.

At the end of January 1954, he left for the Điện Biên Phủ Campaign. He trekked a hundred miles from the Chinese border to Yên Bái, on the Red River, north of Hanoi. From there it was another two hundred miles to the remote valley of Điện Biên Phủ.

Tâm began writing his diary on February 26, 1954, as he set off from Yên Bái with the heavy artillery division to lay siege to the French military fortress.

He confided his thoughts and emotions to his diary. He chronicled in vivid detail the march under fire from French bombers: the teams of Youth Volunteers who built the roads; the units, many of them women, who detonated unexploded bombs to repair the roads; the artillerymen who pulled and dragged two-ton cannons up and down vertiginous slopes; the truck drivers who worked long shifts; and the convoys of bicycles transporting heavy loads of rice to supply the front.

An exhausted Tâm arrived at Điện Biên Phủ a few weeks later, on March 11, happy to ride in a truck for the last mile!

Over the next fifty-five days and nights of the historic Battle of Điện Biên Phủ, between March 13 and May 7, 1954, Tâm was suspended between life and death. He wrote his diary whenever he could, often at night, twenty feet underground next to a cannon, under the stars, or in a quiet place by a stream filled with butterflies.

He lived with the artillerymen. They lacked food, clothes, and sandals, but they surrounded the French military base in the valley without being detected by enemy reconnaissance planes. Under relentless bombings and napalm strikes, they dug bunkers twenty feet deep to hide the

cannons, as well as trenches and tunnels—scooping the earth out with their bare hands to enable the infantry to attack the French positions.

Under enemy fire, Tâm moved around the battlefield, slept at artillery command posts dangerously close to the French forces, and participated in military operations. He transported ammunition, dug underground shelters, and attacked enemy munition depots.

Even though he had spent eight years in the Resistance as a front-line artist-reporter, he was not prepared for the cruelty of the battlefield.

"Were you censored?" I asked.

Tâm laughed at the notion.

"My job was as a reporter for the newspaper. Nobody had the inclination or the time to check up on whether what I was writing was personal or official as long as I did my job!" he answered.

"Did you have a role model?" I asked.

"I admired the Russian war correspondent Ilya Ehrenburg. I wrote with all my heart. I wrote in the style of the time. Socialist realism emphasizes the positive in war, the courage of soldiers, and the camaraderie between us.

"In war there is love and there is hatred. That's what war is. But hatred is not enough to win a war. We had great love; love for our country and love for each other. Those feelings of love are what I expressed in the diary which I carry with me throughout my life.

"There is an aesthetic in war. Because the events you are witnessing are so dreadful, it's up to the artist to use his art to reaffirm life and to communicate his belief in a better future. The French, and later the Americans, burned houses. They burned entire villages."

Tâm believed that through creativity, he retained his humanity and gave hope to others. The glimpse of redemption I had seen in the drawings was not an illusion. Through art, he preserved his sanity, his love of life, and his hope for peace.

"War is so hard. I wanted to make the soldiers feel better by showing them something beautiful. They liked to have me around and to watch

Opposite: Tâm and friends at the entrance of an underground bunker at the Battle of Điện Biên Phủ, 1954. Collection of the artist.

me draw. It seemed to calm them and made them feel special, rather like telling a beautiful girl how beautiful she is.

"In his drawings, the artist must express his love for country and for his fellow soldiers. I never showed hatred in my drawings. Hatred is the inevitable and negative part of war. I wanted to convey uplifting and spiritual feelings, and fragile emotions."

His diary and sketches give a face and a voice to the artillerymen, to the cook who fed them, to the Youth Volunteers who built and repaired the roads, to the civic workers drafted to supply the front, to the political commissars, to the commanders, and to the innocent civilians in the surrounding villages.

Fighting in the trenches with the enemy within eye contact, he imagines too the emotions of the French soldiers, of their commanders, and of the Vietnamese and foreigners fighting on the French side.

The Diary: "I wrote with all my heart."

The diary is a combination of battle notes, interviews, and personal impressions. Tâm's raw, abbreviated style of journalistic notes written on the front line has been preserved in the translation.

Throughout the diary, Tâm expresses a wide range of strong emotions: a patriotic belief in freedom for his homeland, empathy for his comrades-in-arms, sadness at the loss of his friends and a desire to avenge them, and resilience in the face of extreme hardship.

He illustrates with candor the power of propaganda, positive and negative, used to motivate soldiers in war. He also focuses on the concern by commanders, officers, and political commissars for the well-being of their men in order to achieve success, and, in the end, victory over a powerful and superior enemy.

The Artillerymen and Combat Engineers

The artillerymen and combat engineers are the heroes of the diary. The artillerymen hauled cannons up and down steep hills, built bunkers twenty feet underground, and coordinated attacks with the infantry. The combat engineers planned, built, and repaired hundreds of miles of roads to the isolated valley of Điện Biên Phủ, under bombardments

from the French Air Tactical Command.

His lost boys of war, described in Western war propaganda as communist fanatics or robotic killers, are young and innocent. They miss their families and wait with anticipation for letters from home. They fear death and shed tears for their friends. They endure privations with stoicism and humor. They go into battle barefoot. They survive on a single bowl of rice a day and, even hungry, refuse to eat the chocolate they found in the French airdrops, finding it "too bitter!"

The Youth Volunteers

Tâm identifies with the young men and women his age drafted into Youth Volunteer units. The Youth Volunteers were stationed along vertiginous roads at high passes under fire from French bombers.

They built and repaired the roads after the bombings, detonated unexploded ordnance, and filled giant bomb craters, risking their lives to keep the truck convoys moving toward the front.

The trucks transported weapons, ammunition, medicine, rice, and other military supplies to Điện Biên Phủ. The People's Army did not have an air force and relied on transport by foot, bicycle, and truck.

Above: Tâm at Điện Biên Phủ, wearing the
quilted jacket of the soldiers of the Việt Nam
People's Army, 1954. Photographic print.
Collection of the artist.

The Civic Workers

From his time in the Resistance, Tâm felt gratitude for the people who had looked after him in the villages. Thirty thousand civilians were mobilized to join the Điện Biên Phủ Campaign to transport rice, medicines, ammunition, and disassembled weapons. They worked as porters, bicycle and truck drivers, and road builders. Special bicycles adapted with a bamboo pole carried up to two hundred pounds through rough jungle.

Civic workers were unpaid civilians drafted into service. Tâm conveys the dangers and hardship they faced without questioning the practice. Under colonial rule, rural civilians had been forced to supply a month of free labor, the *corvée*, to the occupying power.

Women in War

Women appear in the diary as Youth Volunteers, civic workers, singers in performing arts groups, prostitutes, and civilians.

Gender equality was one of Hồ Chí Minh's political platforms. Tâm

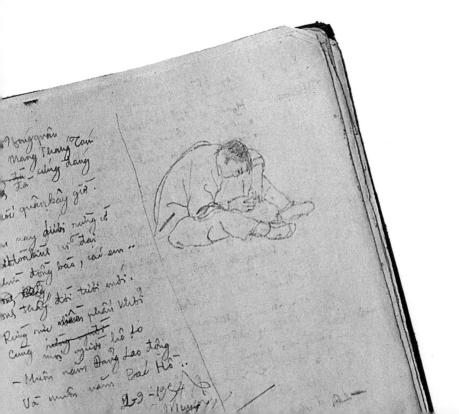

mentions the freedom and equality women have been waiting for "for so long."

There wasn't much time for love in war, but Tâm alludes discreetly to his crush for a singer from a performing arts group.

He drew portraits of Youth Volunteers and tender sketches of Thái civilians in the villages surrounding Điện Biên Phủ.

"One detail to give meaning," he remembered from his teacher in art school, the painter Bùi Xuân Phái:

"I drew a bracelet on the arm of a young girl. The next time I went to her village, she had been killed, burnt beyond recognition. The way I recognized her was because of her bracelet."

The Vietnamese Leaders

Hồ Chí Minh and General Võ Nguyên Giáp were the leading protagonists. Hồ Chí Minh is referred to as "Uncle Hồ," a term of affection and respect. He is portrayed as a benevolent father figure, who is grateful to his flock of young women and men for their sacrifice and martyrdom in the name of the revolution.

General Võ Nguyên Giáp was the strategic mastermind of the Battle of Điện Biên Phủ. He is very present in the diary. His headquarters were close to the front line, and he frequently addressed the troops through letters, instructions, and encouragements. He mixed his exhortations to win with concerns for the soldiers' well-being.

Checked against recently available Vietnamese digital archives, Tâm quotes General Giáp's declarations verbatim. This is a testimony to his journalistic skills under fire.

The Việt Nam People's Army and the Political Commissars

Tâm paints a favorable picture of the political commissars who were the representatives of the Workers' Party (*Đảng lao động Việt Nam*), later renamed the Communist Party. By 1954, the Party was in control of the Việt Minh while non-communist nationalists had been sidelined. On the

Opposite: Facsimile of a diary page with a self-portrait of the author, 1954. Collection of the Điện Biên Phủ Museum.

battlefield, the commissars had the power to override the decisions of combat commanders. They led the men by example, headed up dangerous missions, looked after safety and well-being, and encouraged the men to express concerns in group criticism sessions. At the same time, they kept files on individuals, and enforced strict discipline and harsh punishments.

The Chinese Advisors to the Việt Nam People's Army
Tâm was aware of the presence of Chinese advisors but he considered the subject too sensitive should the diary fall into enemy hands.

The French Commanders and the French Far East Expeditionary Corps
The two main figures of the French Far East Expeditionary Corps were General Henri Navarre, commander-in-chief of the French troops in Indochina, and Colonel Christian de la Croix de Castries.

Navarre selected the remote valley of Điện Biên Phủ to set up a military air base to defend Laos and the Red River Delta against Việt Minh incursions. De Castries was the commander of the eleven-thousand-strong French garrison at Điện Biên Phủ.

Tâm provides context for the men's "hatred" for the occupiers. He cites the French crimes perpetrated over decades of colonial rule: arbitrary killings and detention, torture and rape in the infamous French jails, indiscriminate aerial bombardments, brutal repression of protests, and the great famine.

He acknowledges their respect for French superior military strength. The French had ruled Indochina for close to a hundred years, they sent their most respected generals, de Castries and Navarre, to fight the People's Army, and they were backed by a superpower with unlimited resources: the United States.

When the French capitulation came, Tâm wrote with joy and disbelief: "These infantrymen, these small infantrymen are victorious!"

Opposite: Tâm drawing after the Battle of Điện Biên Phủ, 1954. Photographic print. Collection of the artist.

The Vietnamese Fighting on the French Side
Thirty percent of the French forces were Vietnamese, and twenty percent were "Africans." Tâm considered they were victims of colonialism, and blames the foreign powers for encouraging a civil war. He expresses solidarity with the "Africans"—the Moroccans, Algerians, and Senegalese. He condemns the racism of colonialism and praises the brotherhood among people of color, a cornerstone of the Third Communist International articulated in 1919:
    "The hour of the proletarian dictatorship in Europe will strike for you as the hour of your own emancipation."

The US Military Assistance Advisory Group Indochina
The United States was officially not a party to the war but the Việt Minh were well aware of "secret US" military support. The US Military Assistance Advisory Group Indochina (MAAG) had been established in Saigon in 1950 to administer military aid to the French forces. Tâm lists its chief, John W. O'Daniel, as an advisor. At Điện Biên Phủ, the US provided advisors, pilots, Dakota air planes for airdrops, and napalm, but decided against using nuclear weapons.

"The French and the Americans thought about using nuclear arms on Điện Biên Phủ. Either they didn't have time or they didn't know how to do it without killing French soldiers too. The Americans came to Indochina to help the French. When the American war started, as far as we were concerned, the Americans were already here," he explained.

Prisoners of War

A high proportion of French, Vietnamese, and African prisoners of war interned in jungle camps died in captivity. French sources have been critical of the prisoners' treatment. Recent French sources have recognized that the prisoners were not necessarily mistreated. They received food rations and medical treatment that was equal to what was available to the population around them. But the prisoners were not accustomed to the harsh local wartime conditions and privations.

According to Tâm, the People's Army abided by the 1949 Geneva Conventions in their treatment of prisoners of war. Tâm witnessed the

medical care the prisoners received the day after the capitulation, but he did not follow the fate of the prisoners once they had left Điện Biên Phủ for the jungle internment camps. He also recounts how officers intervened to prevent civic workers from humiliating prisoners of war.

Between the Wars, 1954–1964

On May 7, 1954, the French surrendered. Tâm left the Điện Biên Phủ battlefield a few days later for a military camp in Tuyên Quang Province.

"All I had to do was paint. I was ecstatic. The war was over and I was commissioned by the Army to do a series of watercolors based on my front-line sketches," he remembered.

When news of the 1954 Geneva Accords reached the camp, Tâm was hopeful for peace. But he remained distrustful of US intentions in Indochina when the territory was provisionally divided between the communist DRV (North Vietnam) led by Hồ Chí Minh, and the Republic of Vietnam led by the anti-communist Ngô Đình Diệm (South Vietnam), pending national elections by 1956.

"What did you think?" I asked.

"I had a premonition I would have to go to war again," he replied.

He returned to Hanoi in August 1954. The watercolors based on his combat sketches won third prize at the National Exhibition in October.

In Hanoi, Tâm worked as an illustrator and journalist for *Nhân Dân*, the Communist Party newspaper. In 1963, he enrolled at the Hanoi Institute of Fine Arts to complete his degree.

Two years later in 1965, Tâm's premonition became reality when the United States began a sustained bombing campaign against the DRV, and the first US marines landed in Da Nang to give support to the anti-communist Republic of Vietnam fighting against the National Liberation Front in South Vietnam.

After 1954, Vietnam had remained divided. The national elections for reunification promised by the Geneva Accords never happened, opposed

Opposite: Tâm as an official war artist at the Battle of Khe Sanh in 1968. Khe Sanh was the Điện Biên Phủ of the American Vietnam War (1964–1975). Collection of the artist.

by South Vietnam and the United States who feared a communist victory at the polls by the popular independence hero Hồ Chí Minh.

The division between the communist North and the anti-communist South led directly to the American Vietnam War.

The American Vietnam War, 1964–1975

Tâm returned to the front line as a roving war correspondent and official war artist. In August 1967, he left Hanoi for the long trek down the Ho Chi Minh Trail to the battlefields south of the Demilitarized Zone. Throughout the conflict, he reported on and sketched at the seminal battles of the war in North and South Vietnam.

"What happened to the Điện Biên Phủ diary and sketches?" I wondered.

"Before I left, I had been living in Army barracks in the center of Hanoi. The barracks were housed in a high school that was converted to military use after the students were evacuated to the countryside to escape the bombings.

"I left Hanoi with very little: a backpack, and the same palette and palette knife I used at Điện Biên Phủ. I poured ink into a penicillin vial and put the glass container inside the empty 12.7mm Soviet shell. I even cut the bristles of my toothbrush to make them shorter so I would have room for more paints in my backpack! I wrapped the diary and drawings in plastic, put them in my room, and locked the door. I left the following morning for Khe Sanh, where our troops were preparing for the siege of the US Marine base.

"You never know what's going to happen in war! I didn't know what I'd find when I got back to Hanoi. I went back to my room in the Army barracks. The building was still standing but the soldiers had gone. The place was deserted. I climbed the stairs to the first floor. The lock on the door was broken!

"But I was lucky! The thief had no use for my old things! Everything was still there! You can't imagine how happy I was! It's a miracle they survived!"

The End of Forever War

My last meeting with Tâm was in 2015. His hope was that his diary would be published in Vietnam.

His wish was realized when the Kim Đồng Publishing House in Hanoi published the Vietnamese-language edition on May 7, 2024 to commemorate the seventieth anniversary of the victory of Điện Biên Phủ and fifty years of peace in Vietnam.

As I was revising the introduction for the Vietnamese edition and for the new English-language paperback, I watched the artist Menna Hamouda on social media. The twenty-year-old Palestinian artist painted the resistance of the people of Gaza on the rubble of buildings bombed by the occupying power.

I thought of the young Phạm Thanh Tâm painting on the walls of the ruins of village houses in the French-occupied zone during his days in the Resistance.

Dehumanizing the enemy leads to endless war.

I have the hope that, through his diary and sketches, Phạm Thanh Tâm's humanity, love of life, resilience, and hope under fire will be shared with the younger generations for whom he fought.

Sherry Buchanan
Editor and Publisher
Asia Ink, London
May 7, 2024

Overleaf: Facsimile of pages from Tâm's diary, featuring a hand-drawn map of the Điện Biên Phủ Battlefield, 1954, 22 x 28cm. Collection of the Điện Biên Phủ Museum.

Lai Châu Road

Mường Thanh

Airfield

PH

Bridge

Nậm Rốm River

Route 41

Hill A1

Hills C

Hill D

Hills E

Him Lam

Bản Tầu Village

Độc Lập

E
S ✦ N
W

Kilometer 76 marker

Bến Tre Infantry Division

Artillery Division 351

Artillery Company 804

Artillery Company 806

The Artist on the Battlefield: Map of Điện Biên Phủ
(preceding pages)

Positions of the Việt Nam People's Army
The Việt Nam People's Army under the command of General Võ Nguyên Giáp numbered fifty-three thousand and eight hundred combat and logistics personnel, with several infantry divisions, an artillery division, but no air power and no tanks.

con số 76	Kilometer 76 marker on Route 41
Bến Tre	Infantry Division 312
351	Engineer-Artillery Division 351
806	Artillery Company 806 Howitzers 105mm
804	Artillery Company 804 Howitzers 105mm
	C804 artillerymen were Tâm's friends.
	They trained together in a military camp
	in southwest China.
Lai Châu Dương	Lai Châu Road, People's Army supply road
Dương 41	Route 41, People's Army supply road
Bản Tấu	Thái village bombed with napalm

Positions of the French Far East Expeditionary Corps
The French forces under the command of Colonel Christian de Castries numbered eleven thousand combat and logistics personnel, with heavy artillery including 155mm cannons, air power, and tanks. Two airfields supplied the military base.

Mường Thanh	Valley of Điện Biên Phủ
PH	French Headquarters (HQ)
Sân bay	French airstrip
] [	Iron bridge
Nậm Rốm	River that runs through the valley
Độc Lập	French stronghold Gabrielle
Him Lam	French stronghold Béatrice
D	Hill D, French stronghold Dominique 2
e	Hill E, French stronghold Dominique 1
C	Hill C, French stronghold Eliane 1

A1   Hill A1, French stronghold Eliane 2

Hồng Cúm, the French stronghold Isabelle, was five miles to the south of the French HQ and had an airstrip. Hồng Cúm, which is not represented on the map, resisted until the French capitulation on May 7.

Phạm Thanh Tâm's Itinerary Around the Battlefield

March 11	At Kilometer 76, "we turned at a big banyan tree, followed a steep path for a little over a mile, then drove slightly uphill to reach the firing line."
March 12–21	At the headquarters of Artillery Division 351.
March 13	First artillery barrage.
March 21–28	On the move with the 105mm Howitzer company, C804, to a new position a mile and a half from Hill D.
March 30	At C804 new command post. Second artillery barrage.
April 12	At the anti-aircraft command post C228, near Độc Lập Hill with the artillerymen who shot down the fiftieth plane at Điện Biên Phủ near Độc Lập Hill.
April 13	Tấu village.
April 14	At the command post of the anti-aircraft defense companies C228 and C227, near Độc Lập.
April 16–May 4	At the headquarters of Artillery Division 351.
May 1	Third artillery barrage.
May 4–6	At the mountain artillery command posts on Hills D and E.
May 7	At the mountain artillery command post on Hill E. General Attack.

On the Road

"We were young, but our faces were old."
Phạm Thanh Tâm begins his diary in the winter of 1954 when he joins the Điện Biên Phủ Campaign, the greatest offensive of the war.

The young artist-reporter works for the newspaper of the heavy artillery division of the People's Army. He is traveling with a performing arts team sent to entertain the troops at the front.

Tâm advances under heavy enemy bombardment through one of the most punishing jungles in the world. "Exhausted," he finally comes to a gravel road, part of the six-hundred-mile network built and motorized by the People's Army to reach the inaccessible valley of Điện Biên Phủ.

The French command never imagined that the People's Army would transport heavy artillery to besiege the remote French military fortress.

Tâm carries with him a backpack, a rice belt, and his most precious possessions: his notebook, his pen, and his inkwell. He has carefully covered the notebook with a piece of indigo-blue cloth, cut from his shirt, to protect it against the humidity of the Tonkin region.

He sketches soldiers on their way to the front, artillerymen hauling cannons, workers carrying supplies to the front, and the young men and women building the roads.

Tâm's colorful watercolors mirror his hope for a free Vietnam, while his dark sketches in charcoal convey the cruelty of armed resistance and war.

Opposite:
Tâm's pen, inkwell, and notebook, 1954, 22 x 14cm.
Collection of the Điện Biên Phủ Museum.

Above, a soldier gives a last look to the forlorn figure of his beloved as he leaves for the front. A People's Army helmet on his head, carrying a backpack and rice belt, he cuts a solitary figure against a dark and menacing background. Tâm, for all his youthful enthusiasm, like the soldier in his drawing, enters a foreboding mental and physical landscape as he nears the valley of Điện Biên Phủ.

Could the People's Army, with no air force and no tanks, prevail against a superior force in their fight for independence from colonial rule?

(**Editor's Note:** Text in italic and regular text between brackets have been provided by the Editor for context.)

February 21, 1954

From the Ngọc Pier[1] ferry crossing on the River Chảy to the town of Yên Bái on the Red River (18 miles; ETA on foot: 6 hours).

I leave for the campaign. I'm happy and enthusiastic because I feel healthy, but I'm a bit skinny. I'm traveling on foot with half of the performing arts team [of the Engineer-Artillery Division 351].[2]

By the ferry crossing at the Ngọc Pier on the River Chảy,[3] it was already afternoon. The French enemy bombed a few days ago. Ngọc town has lost its joy because of the destruction of bricks and tiles. The red soil is gouged and dug into large puddles. Palm trees are truncated, leaving behind ragged, yellowing, and sullen branches.

In the afternoon, the water was flowing fast. Like every afternoon, a flock of white storks flew back to the North, whitening the entire river.

Crossing the Red River[4] in Yên Bái Province[5]

We went all around the town of Yên Bái. The zone at the rear of the campaign is happy. People are cheerful. The harvest has been good; rice production has increased; streets and markets are crowded with people buying and selling … children are dressed in colorful clothes, and mill about freely, unafraid. In the evening, students in the town library read copies of *The Sharp Knife Brigade*. They boast and dream about living the heroic life of soldiers fighting the enemy.

Fresh papaya is especially abundant! The large, ripe fruits are everywhere in the shops and markets. [My friend] Lan and I have been craving papaya for a long time, we ate three or four papayas at once!

We slept at Thạch's friend's house. Thạch already has a baby, being cradled in her mother's arms. He looks so mature now, like a husband and father. His father-in-law was so happy to see young soldiers; he went to the garden to pick papaya, and cut sugarcane for us.

Opposite: The soldier's farewell, 1954, charcoal on paper, 20 x 15cm. Collection of the artist.
Overleaf: After a bombing raid, no date, watercolor on paper, 16 x 24cm. Collection of the artist.

February 22, 1954
From Yên Bái on the Red River to the Lũng Lô Pass.[6] *Route 13*[7] *was the People's Army's main supply route to Điện Biên Phủ.*[8] *The French Air Force dropped twelve thousand tons of bombs on the mountain pass in an effort to disrupt supplies (40 miles; ETA on foot: 15 hours).*

Crossed the Red River today
As we reached the river's wide, sandy beach, Thu, the "kid doctor," was homesick. He was thinking of his father who lives on the left bank of the Thao River, the mainstream of the Red River in Phú Thọ Province. Thu is only seventeen. He works as a paramedic and nurse on the road. He's everybody's younger brother, especially our comrade Viện who is in his forties. Thu has a bright smile, round face, and dimples in his cheeks. He often calls out to Viện:
"Hey Dad! Dad!"

On Route 13
A strong and cool northwest wind blows toward the east. Every stone, every step of this road is the sweat and blood of our people and soldiers, determined to pave the way to the campaign.

The new road to Điện Biên Phủ is several hundred miles long.[9] It is being built in secret, over a long period of time, with the strength of human hands and will, moving forward step by step through the newly liberated zone.

We no longer have to take shortcuts through the jungle.

We have faith:

"Traffic flow is guaranteed!"

Up the Lũng Lô Pass
Youth Volunteers[10] wear the warm, green, cotton-padded jackets of the People's Army: men and women smile and encourage each other on this dangerous stretch of road, far up the Lũng Lô Pass. *Clin clan* sounds are fast and strong but accurate, hitting huge rocks on cliffs, constructing temporary bridges over abysses ... Building a public road as though it was their own ... Why not, since the road is ours! Who could have brought voices and laughter from the lowlands by the sea trapped in the

enemy zone to these high mountain peaks and deep valleys if not the Resistance war, Uncle Hồ,[11] and the Vietnamese Labor Party?

... But look ... out of breath and overwhelmed after the climb ... the mountain was split in half, the gravel road went right through the entire mountain ... the civic workers broke rocks with their hands and simple tools to pave the way ... the scenery was spectacular!

Thought of Uncle Hồ's poem:

Nothing is difficult
Only fear that your heart will not persevere
Dig mountains and fill in seas
You can do it if you have the will.

On the road to Điện Biên Phủ, 1954,
watercolor on paper, 35 x 25cm.
Collection of the artist.

Above: *Portrait of a Youth Volunteer,* 1954,
watercolor on paper, 30 x 23cm.
Opposite: *Woman carrying dried rice cakes,*
1954, ink and wash on paper, 25 x 14cm.

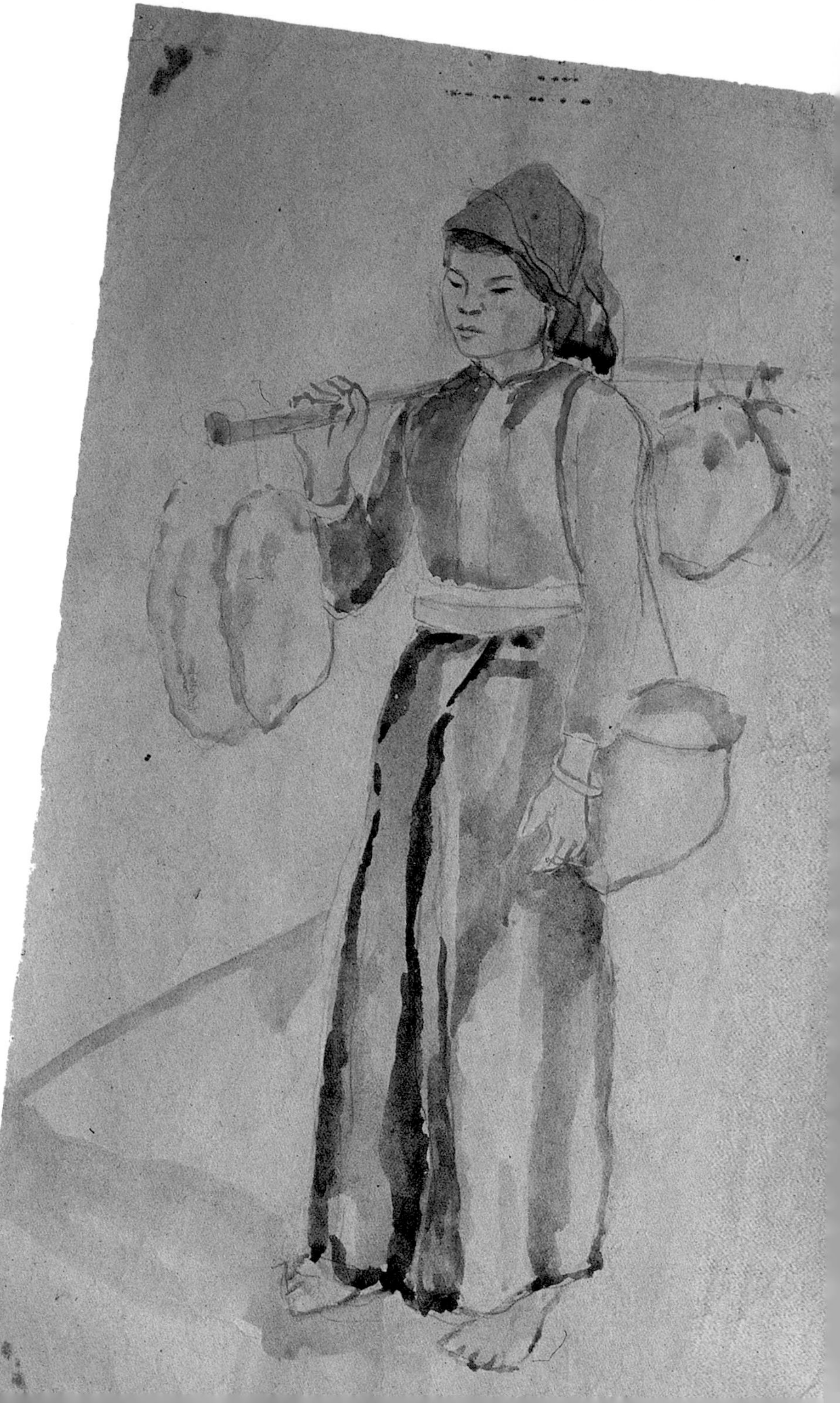

February 27, 1954

From the Lũng Lô Pass and the Black River to the valley of Cò Nòi (64 miles; ETA on foot: 24 hours).

Along the way, I met civic workers[12] [porters and bicycle drivers who supply the front] from Vĩnh Phúc Province,[13] a zone temporarily occupied by the enemy. The young women in the group were turned down at first, but then allowed to join. When they were accepted, they wanted to go, but they missed home. They had never carried forty-five-pound loads up steep slopes. It made them cry but they got used to it.

Living in the enemy zones, these civic workers didn't believe it when they heard that here, in the liberated zones, roads are being widened and there are cars ...

They're happy to see that our forces have grown. They're learning politics, patriotic songs, and dances ... Especially women from the farms feel liberated from old customs ... they've craved freedom for so long.

At a recent festival, provincial teams all contributed artistic revolutionary performances. But Vĩnh Phúc had nothing. They ask soldiers to teach them patriotic songs and dances:

... D G G A E B ... (*Re Sol Sol La Mi Si*)

Vĩnh Phúc was recently awarded over ten Third Class Soldier Medals and an honorary flag from Uncle Hồ.

Exploits include:

A forty-seven-year-old civilian worker carried one hundred pounds and a sick colleague for six miles.

Mr Duy, from Lâm Thao, Phú Thọ, carried one hundred and ninety pounds—he's a champion.

Truck drivers have been driving for four months without a day off. They work eighteen hours a day. Another group of civic workers has been on the road for over six months. They're overdue for [home leave] but they've stayed on to continue working. They're homesick. They're afraid their homeland will be invaded by the enemy ... slogans on billboards [at the rest stations] keep up their spirits:

"Determined to serve the campaign until victory!"

"The soldiers on the front line (Điện Biên Phủ) are waiting for us!"

"Old lady" planes[14] have been more active these last few days: planes fly back and forth, one after another, from the front to the rear ... Who the hell cares? Down here we're working, dancing. Trucks are picking up rice [for the front] from the small warehouses on the edge of the jungle ... [sometimes] they explode and catch fire.

It's a bit difficult to cook ... have to be careful about the smoke and the light from cooking fires ... loading rice at night until dawn. The sound echoed through the jungle.

I met civic workers with water bamboo pipes.[15] I asked for a puff but they refused. Lucky I found pipes at the rest station further on for anyone to smoke.

A father and son were together in a platoon. The sixteen-year-old boy wanted to continue [to the front] but couldn't. He was crying. He tapped on a gas tank, pretending it was a frog drum.[16]

One more day before we cross the Black River.[17]

We stopped for a rest in the jungle.

I went to a festival for pack bicycle drivers[18] from Phú Thọ. They call themselves "Little Motorbikes."

We sat in a rice storage depot like in a plane. The walls were decorated with nylon and candy wraps. Three small photos of the leaders hung beside a flag from the "Supply the Front" Council of Việt Nam, and a "Determined to Win to Get Uncle Hồ's Flag" banner. We shared candy, honey cakes, and oranges. We had spring water to drink.

The lights in the festival warehouse were powered by two spinning bicycle dynamos.

The warehouse was turned into a stage. Men and women from the performing arts unit joined in dancing and singing. It was fun and very moving. We sang:

Bring rice to everyone
Go to the battlefield to kill the colonialists
... take camouflage leaves
... a load of rice, a box of ammunition
Let our soldiers defeat the enemy
Lalalalala ... *tình tính tang* ... contributes to victory.

The pack bicycle drivers compete among themselves. The standard load is one hundred and seventy to two hundred pounds. Mr Tú carried

four hundred pounds (double the normal load). And I heard that Mr Thuyết from Bắc Giang Province[19] transported five hundred pounds. Pack bicycles are strengthened by adding metal, wood, or bamboo struts to regular bicycles. The Phú Thọ bicycle drivers won a Latin American flag from ICRAF (an international agro-forestry organization). The delegation from Thái Nguyên,[20] determined to get the flag, challenged the winners.

Crossing the Black River

The sound of canoes rattling alongside the ferry. In the afternoon, the green mountains were reflected in the still waters of the river. It's the

A soldier smoking a bamboo water pipe at night, 1954,
charcoal on paper, 26 x 36cm. Private collection.

dry season. In the distance, streaks of slash-and-burn fires stretch across the high mountains, where the Mèo live in scattered houses.[21]

Evening. We're about to cross the river. The convoy of pack bicycles hurtled down the slope; wooden brakes creaked. A thin streak of light shone down to the dock from a bicycle light above. Several boats flickered with night lights … sounds of laughter on the river. Suddenly, the twin-fuselage plane that had been flying loudly above us all day in the hot sun flew past again. All the lights went out. The canoes fell silent.

I met a group of Youth Volunteers mostly from farming and *petit bourgeois* families. Their faces are young, they play innocently, they really want to wear our Army uniform. The legal age to join up is eighteen to twenty-five—but many lie about their age, and are sixteen, seventeen.

On the road

I'm getting used to the noise of enemy planes and the harsh sunlight on the road. My heart softened with the greeting laughter of young women civic workers, going in the opposite direction.

[Yesterday] afternoon, I was about to cross the Black River. I was walking briskly. I bumped into a pack bicycle loaded with rice. The bicycle fell over, twisting the wheels. I was stunned, wondering … before I could apologize or figure out what to do, the drivers gathered round. They were very cordial.

"Don't worry, keep going. We'll fix it and rebalance the rim," they said.

I thanked them and ran to catch up with the performing arts group.[22] I feel guilty in my heart. These guys will have to stop to fix that pack bicycle, it will take a lot of time … and it's already dark!

We arrived at a beautiful valley near Cò Nòi[23] with rolling hills and big trees. But one area was filthy: withered grass, messy piles of old cans, and barbed wire—it was the old enemy post.

March 2, 1954
From Cò Nòi to Nà Sản (12.5 miles; ETA on foot: 4 hours 30).[24]

On to Hát Lót. Then Nà Sản: the old French air base was deserted …

March 5, 1954
From Nà Sản to Sơn La (12 miles; ETA on foot: 4 hours 30).[25]

Arrived in Sơn La. The French barracks and their brick houses on the hill were destroyed, a few walls were left standing. A flamboyant tree, its long, wilted fruits were scattered around, amid piles of dirty, empty cans.

We're staying at a house near the town. The villagers have fled and

the place is deserted. The tamarind tree is full of ripe fruit. A stream flows by, meandering. I peeled the tamarind fruits and pressed them into a water pipe ... a refreshing dessert for the upcoming march.

March 6, 1954
From Sơn La to the Pha Đin Pass (40 miles; ETA on foot: 16 hours).[26]

It's another fifty miles to the junction at Tuần Giáo (Sơn La, Lai Châu, and Điện Biên Phủ). But first, I mentally have to prepare myself to climb the steep Pha Đin Pass! The pass is twenty miles long. Pha means sky, Đin means earth to the Thái[27] in the northwest ... between Heaven and Earth!

High mountains, steep slopes ... Hard and dangerous! ... But spring lingers in the jungle with white streaks of *ban* flowers![28] Now I understand the beauty of the "white forest of trees in flower." Each white flower has a pink pistil in the middle; its leaves appear in pairs, like blue butterfly wings playing with the white flowers. The bark is dry and dark, blending in with the background so that only the white color stands out, the most beautiful trees in the jungle!

We reached the top of the Pha Đin Pass.

Mr Thụy, commander of the engineer regiment, is in charge:[29]

"This pass zigzags and makes it difficult to build bridges. Wood and bamboo we need for construction are far from here. The engineers have wrestled with this mountain pass for the past three months. It's ten miles from the rest station to their work area to open the bypass. Sometimes they work twenty hours a day.

"The French broadcast on the radio that the pass is a key choke point. It's a massive concentration of destruction. Thirty planes drop one hundred and two bombs a day: B24s, B26s[30] and Hellcats.[31] From December 6 to 16, 1953, they dropped twelve time-bombs every night, as well as butterfly bombs[32] (which contain seventy bomblets). During the first week in January 1954, they dropped six bombs a day.

Opposite: Fighter (Chiến sĩ), Điện Biên Phủ, 1954,
ink and wash on paper, 16 x 10.5cm. Collection
of the Ho Chi Minh City Fine Arts Museum.

"Seven to fourteen bombs hit the road during any given bombing, along a one-mile stretch. That's three thousand cubic meters of soil to fill in. The engineers repair the road. The soil is like powder, wherever we dig to clear the road, butterfly bombs explode … "

Special road opening for General Võ Nguyên Giáp[33]

Mr Thụy, commander of the engineer company, continued:

"It took three nights for the regiment and one night for the General to get through the pass.

"One hundred engineer soldiers worked fifty hours straight. They cleared over three thousand cubic meters of soil. Each cleared twenty cubic meters (on the special night General Võ Nguyên Giáp came through the pass). One platoon filled a bomb crater with ninety cubic meters of soil in forty-five minutes. Another filled two bomb craters in three hours.

"Comrade Kim, a squadron officer, volunteered to walk in front, holding a six-and-a-half-foot-long stick (can't be any longer) ready to sacrifice himself—banging on branches to shake off butterfly bombs and detonate them (Comrade Kim was promoted to deputy platoon commander). Luckily, the bombs that fell on the road detonated.

"The platoon officers have been exemplary. The engineers were determined to get the bomb disposal work done by 2 a.m. Nobody expected they could do it. There were time-delayed bombs every ten to fifteen feet.

"A bomb exploded. Some brothers were buried. When they were pulled from the rubble, Comrade Châu said:

—I'm fine, sir!

"Comrade Như (a new recruit) fainted. The blast threw him from the upper to the lower road. When he came to, he said:

—Tomorrow I'll come back to continue fighting!

"Comrade Hoa, the sub-commander, and Khiển, the deputy platoon leader, were buried. The company commander dug them out. Let us continue our mission, they said. The company commander told them they needed to rest … One officer was hit by huge chunks of earth and was in terrible pain, but didn't make a sound. Someone started to sing over the explosions:

'Bombs are feudal and colonial ... Explosions, instant or delayed, will not stop us from building the roads!'

"We advise the brothers to be cautious, don't be careless. Being subjective—confusing butterfly bombs with time-bombs—can mean death.

"One butterfly bomb luckily was in position two, so it didn't explode immediately. The sappers in charge calmly reported it to the officer."

Additional notes:

A new recruit defused fifty butterfly bombs in one night.

A reconnaissance team was close by when a time-bomb exploded ten feet away; the five-hundred-pound bomb exploded very loudly ... the weak-spirited would have easily panicked ...

Observation soldiers keep a calm mind,[34] wait for the bombs to fall, watch for the exact drop points, and then take cover.

A delegation of high-level cadres came through the pass. Brothers volunteered to search for unexploded bombs during dangerous hours to get the road cleared in time. The platoon commanders were exemplary, digging up and defusing bombs (selfless, ready for sacrifice!). The vehicles got through the pass before midnight, the commanders fulfilled their mission. The bombed road section was at the top of the pass, the unit's garrison is five miles away, at the bottom of the pass.

The engineers work at night ... when enemy planes drop bright flares, they flatten themselves against the cliff. When the flares stop, they start digging again without torches. One-thousand-pound bombs[35] target our observation posts: enemy planes drop six bombs a day.

Right-thinking is very important. Soldiers, in some cases, encourage their squadron officers:

"Why don't you go ahead?"

Engineer soldiers care for one another: after an explosion, they search for teammates, dig them out, and act quickly to save them.

"We don't have enough nurses, but we're used to it: people with minor injuries carry those with serious injuries on stretchers," Comrade Hoa told me.

The Pha Đin Pass is a very important strategic point on the way to attack Điện Biên Phủ. The People's Army newspaper has named the engineer unit: "Tiger of Pha Đin Pass."

I asked Mr Thụy, the company commander:

"What do you think is the basis for your determination?"

"There are times when we're afraid of death, but because of our responsibility to everyone, and for the success of the Điện Biên Phủ Campaign ... we're required to try our best. And I have great faith in the ability of every engineer in our unit," he answered.

Additional notes:

Comrades Định the platoon leader, Định the political officer, and Thụy are exemplary and brave.

Comrade Như was injured. When he regained consciousness, he laughed. Then passed out from the pain.

News came on Saturday night, while the unit was out in the field: the High Command awarded the unit a First Class Soldier Medal and Uncle Hồ's flag.

March 8, 1954

From the Pha Đin Pass to the Kilometer 76 marker on Route 41,[36] a mile from the headquarters of Artillery Division 351 (55 miles; ETA on foot: 20 hours).

Tâm meets up with his friends Quý and the C804 gunners he trained with in China.[37] They reveal that, in January 1954, they hauled the 105mm cannons[38] into position, ready to attack the French military fortress. But they were abruptly ordered to withdraw, no questions asked! General Giáp later wrote in his memoirs that the decision to order a withdrawal and postpone the battle was "the hardest decision of my entire life as a military commander ... Hauling the guns had been painful, but hauling them back out was worse."[39]

Opposite: Men hauling a two-ton cannon uphill, ink sketch on rice paper, 14 x 16cm.
Overleaf: Pulling the cannon to Điện Biên (Tôi kéo pháo Điện Biên), ink sketch on paper, 14 x 16cm.

All along the road, we met engineers, civic workers, Youth Volunteers. The road and the mountains are red with bomb craters as we get closer to the front line. The villages are empty. People have fled to live deep in the jungle.

Our artillery took control of the battlefield for the first time in January 1954.

[An artilleryman told me:]

"At the Kilometer 70 marker on the Lai Châu Road. Not prepared for difficulties. On the first day, officers went with the battalion and found the way [to haul the artillery to besiege the French military fortress] wasn't easy. Artillerymen were encouraged to make ropes, two ropes per platoon [ten to twelve gunners]; each rope was fifty feet long.

"Dark, bushy, hard to pass, stumbling over trees and rivers …

"Pulling the guns uphill:

—Two … three!"

"Going downhill: four-thousand-pounds [each gun weighed one thousand pounds or half a ton] … Number 4. Numbers 5 and 6 were tired, they bent, weak, as though their bones were broken.

"On the second day, someone had the idea to put grass under the guns so the artillerymen didn't have to carry them.

"On the fourth day, they were overtired, but there were two more sixty-five degree slopes—the battery heads shouted:

—Two … three …

"Numbers 1 and 5 wedged themselves in, but they kept being hit in the face by the cannon wheel. The infantry came to their aid; even so, they advanced only two and a half miles that night.

"Numbers 7, 9, 10, 1, 8 were absent; there were only six gunners and seventy infantrymen left …

"Going downhill, the winches broke: the gun thundered down. Xích and three gunners held on and steered the wheels to a flat place to prevent it from falling into a river …

"On the fifth day, only one more slope to reach a flat area, the winches broke again … the five gunners who were left and the infantrymen … determined not to be discouraged … And they kept the gun safe.

"They stayed for a day. The artillery platoon hadn't reinforced the fortifications when they received the order to withdraw:

—Pull the guns out … "

"Exhausted!

—Why did they say we would withdraw by truck? everyone wondered.

"During the withdrawal: Enemy cannons fired from three hundred feet away. It was dangerous. The artillery kept moving through the night, no sleep in the morning. The infantry brothers were angry. Bamboo trees cracked … stayed patient and encouraged each other. It was tough going all through the night. Next to jungle, next to deep rivers. Sometimes the enemy shelled from thirty feet away. Do they know where were are? Enemy shells exploded, violent booms. Our gunners and infantrymen ignored them. They didn't leave the artillery.

—Heave now and heave hard …

"Hauling guns, up and down … Past an old hill, dark, burned by napalm bombs.[40]

"An 'old lady' flew low down …

—Hurry up!

—Two, three … hey!

—Battery 2 has casualties!

—The injured must leave the battlefield!

"During the day, the artillerymen worried the big guns were exposed … there were no underground shelters, bombs exploded nearby.

"Artillery pieces barreled down the slope again! A hundred and thirty feet down! Very determined and brave, gunners and infantry steered the guns to safety. (The political commissar[41] and the infantry gave praise: The artillery and the infantry work well together! The relationship between artillery and infantry has never been closer! The Party and people have entrusted these precious guns. Infantry and artillery really need each other. So many battles when the infantry needed guns and there were none … Come on, hold on, come on—our artillery!)

"Exhausted bodies, stomachs cramping, blurred vision … they kept hauling the guns out of position … Enemy fire pursued them … Shells exploded all around them. Enemy planes bombed. Six comrades were injured in one battery: Tạo, Như, Dãn, Phức … a soldier from the gun-carriage unit was seriously hurt. His arms were broken, his intestines were punctured; Hiện's leg was injured.

"Alive or dead, the gunners held on to steer the wheels … until the gun trailers arrived and the trucks towed them away … "

It took them seven days to haul the guns over twelve miles of mountainous terrain.

The unit received the Third Class Military Merit Medal.

Building the battlefield, January 1954

Quý from C804, told me:

"We had been hauling the guns on mountain paths for five miles. We were surprised to meet engineers and infantrymen.

—Artillery officers, they whispered.

"We had almost reached the fields of Tấu village, two miles from the enemy, but we had no intelligence about the enemy yet ...

"In the evening, a reconnaissance unit, with infantry support crossed the Lai Châu Road down to a war-torn field. Nobody in sight.

"The mountain villages were completely deserted. Only buffaloes, scattered straw[42] and rice, bomb craters. A buffalo lay dead, rotting. Early in the morning, a few villagers returned home, and quickly disappeared again.

"We decided to build the C804 battlefield in the middle of the field.

"The following night, the engineers came to help.

"On the first day, we carried the guns to the battlefield.

"The next night, enemy shells poured down on us. We were crossing a field carrying wood back from the jungle ... we lay down. They stopped shooting, we began to advance again. Enemy bullets exploded on the road, in the river ... some brothers were killed.

"Battery 4 dug the underground shelter on low-lying land. It filled up with water.

"The next night, we dug the underground shelter in a new place ... The officers stayed up all night. They got a couple of hours' sleep the next day ... Reconnaissance and observation units carried out topographic surveys during the day, and helped dig underground fortifications at night.

"Tịnh led a topographic unit in the small hours of the morning when the dew is on leaves. They were spotted by an enemy plane, by villagers (and spies) ... they were shelled by enemy cannons shortly after. Xuất lay flat on the ground, holding onto the surveying equipment ... When the enemy stopped firing, he got up to continue the survey ... The enemy fired again ... fierce, he led his unit back into the jungle.

"After building the shelters, we received the order to withdraw.

"Hauling guns again with more than a hundred people. Going downhill, the battery commander was the guy in front. We were unable to hold the cannon, the wheels flipped over.

"On the way back during the withdrawal, we saw a village. There was nobody there, but a fire was burning.

"While pulling these two tons of precious steel up and down the slope under enemy fire, the gunners and infantrymen shouted:

—Even dead, never let go of the ropes! Never leave the wheels!

"Battery 2 was exhausted. They hauled the artillery pieces up the slope, within range of enemy fire. Great effort, but by 6 a.m. they hadn't reached the top! They tried to hide the guns.

"We had nothing to use as camouflage, except reeds. We tied the reeds into bunches, and hoped the camouflage would blend in with the devastated surroundings.

"We hid in a small underground shelter ... an 'old lady' spotted us, we were engulfed by enemy fire ... Nghĩa, Tý, and Lộc lay down, their eyes on the guns.

"A blockbuster bomb fell sixty feet from the cannon. Luckily, nothing happened. The deputy leader ran down.

"The brigade called and asked:

—Is everything okay?

"The guns weren't spotted thanks to careful camouflage. An infantry comrade was killed by enemy fire. Everyone held onto the ropes. We got the artillery safely back to the main road. Trucks waited for the artillery coming down the slope and towed them away.

A truck broke down within range of enemy fire. We helped the driver push the truck and he drove out of range.

"We held a meeting in a shelter. Discussed our experience, and praised individual records."

When Quý left the meeting, he saw a gunner lying on the roadside wrapped in a blanket. It was Phức. His foot had been crushed by the cannon. Quý was moved and offered to carry him. Phức refused.

"Don't worry, I can drag my leg!" he said.

Phức bandaged his foot and found a safe place to rest.

Additional notes:
Guns can be hauled with good ropes.
  Haul the guns at night.
  During the day, chop logs, fetch reeds, and make ropes.
  During withdrawal, camouflage the cannons for several miles.
C804 was awarded a Third Class Medal for pulling the cannons for twelve miles in seven days.

Tâm meets the commander of the artillery regiment that carried out a diversionary mission in Upper Laos.[43] *General Giáp, after postponing the start date for the attack against Điện Biên Phủ, in January 1954, launched an offensive in Upper Laos to divert the French forces away from Điện Biên Phủ while his troops withdrew.*

❦

Comrade Nguyễn Đình, the commander of Artillery Regiment 675,[44] told me about the mission in Upper Laos:

"Some brothers were wrong to say:

—When you come you have fat, when you leave you have bones.

"The soldiers were building trenches when they were ordered to withdraw.

—Whatever the superiors say, we'll do it, no more questions ... some said.

"Others wondered:

—Have we been discovered? Is that why we have to withdraw?

—Why don't we attack them?

"During the operation, the unit had very little food for nine days: a lạng[45] of rice a day mixed with cassava, vegetables, and wild spinach.[46]

"Bad: Some soldiers ate big rice balls, and fetched more cooked rice and dry food from the kitchen.

"Good: The people gave the soldiers canned food, sticky rice ... but the soldiers didn't eat it. They stuck to the rules.[47]

"Soldiers wrote revolutionary poems encouraging self-discipline.

"Platoon officers Nhượng and Thủng ate half a rice ball each, and gave the other half to the soldiers.

"Hùng the company commander, Chấn the political commissar, and platoon and squadron officers Hộ, Bổng, Năng, Kiên, and Thủng shared the soldiers' heavy loads, and showed concern for their health (good positive propaganda work).

"We crossed fifty mountain passes. Each pass was half a mile long. We were exhausted, carrying heavy loads ... we were so happy when we got the order to attack the enemy from a high slope.

"Climbing six hours up and down rocky mountain paths, the brothers cut wood in the forest to build quick but sturdy fortifications. We built six fortifications in two days.

"We shot three enemy planes, two "old ladies," one Dakota![48]

"We fired continuously at the enemy artillery.

"When we returned: we were awarded a Third Class Military Merit Medal, a pig, and food by the Command Unit (Laos).

"We learned the meaning and purpose of the victory of the Upper Laos Campaign. We mobilized the Lao people, cared for wounded soldiers, and promoted solidarity between artillery and infantry, and a good relationship between officers and soldiers.

"Soldiers asked:

—Why don't we liberate the people of Laos since we eat their food?

"New recruits who thought it was easy to attack the enemy artillery lost confidence when there were difficulties … "

"Company 113 reported:

—While advancing, we were ordered to withdraw to Cháy Hill.

Some brothers were upset and said:

—Retreat to Cháy Hill and then withdraw to Tuyên Quang?[49]

"Some didn't believe in the fighting determination of our unit and of the local regiment.

"Marching through Upper Laos, we heard that a unit at Điện Biên Phủ had resolved the post we intended to attack; we were worried that our unit would be withdrawn from the fighting.

"During the fight against the enemy in Mường Khoa, some soldiers thought of looting.

"Good: Some soldiers are sick or have sore feet … there are no bandages, so they tied rags around their feet and continued carrying the guns.

"We organized festivals, promoted Vietnamese–Laotian solidarity, and mobilized the Lao to support Prime Minister Prince Souphanouvong [a Việt Minh ally].[50]

We ate rice with salt, saving the meat for the boatmen …

Laos people love Vietnamese soldiers."

March 10, 1954

Tâm boards a truck at the Kilometer 76 marker for the short distance to the headquarters of Artillery Division 351, his destination at Điện Biên Phủ.

I heard on the radio news that we destroyed eighteen enemy planes at Gia Lâm [Hanoi Airport], and sixty at Cát Bi–Haiphong Airport. French and American pilots[51] were at the airports.

At 3:30 a.m., I got on a truck with my group. It's starting to be called the front line, a few miles from the enemy. The truck was packed. But it was better than carrying heavy loads and climbing up steep slopes on foot! The headlights flashed white over long stretches in the dense foggy night.

Our soldiers are ready to attack the enemy at "Trần Đình," code-name for Điện Biên Phủ!

Our mottos:

"Steady Attack. Steady Advance!"[52]

"Fight persistently, with determination!"

At the Kilometer 76 marker, we turned right at a big banyan tree, followed a steep trail for a mile, then drove uphill to reach the artillery division command headquarters.

All units have a code name:

Hải Lăng Regiment 45[53]

Long Châu Division 351[54]

Châu Giang Regiment 675[55]

Bến Tre (infantry): "Increase labor productivity."[56]

The artillery bunkers[57] are halfway up a high mountain. The brothers who arrived first have been digging.

Enemy planes roar.

Order to open fire at 3 a.m. [tomorrow night]!

Above: Vietnamese troops pulling cannons into Điện Biên Phủ, 1954. Photographic archive of the *People's Army Newspaper*.

In the Trenches

The attack by the People's Army against the formidable French military fortress is only days away. An excited and anxious Tâm spends his first nights at Điện Biên Phủ in the bunker of the artillery division headquarters where the newspaper is printed, "soil trickling down my neck, and mud in my hair."

Over the next fifty-five days and nights, the intrepid reporter moves around the battlefield under enemy fire, through trenches and minefields. He records battles and interviews artillerymen on the front line.

He captures the raw emotions of young kids off the farm, with little training, using second-hand artillery, facing a superior army: their bravery, their fear of death, their love for one another, their desire to avenge loved ones and comrades, and their suffering.

But even after eight years of war, Tâm is unprepared for the loss of life he witnesses at Điện Biên Phủ. He writes that he has hardened his heart. The poignancy of his sketches and drawings testify to the solace he found in art.

The first phase of the battle started on March 13, 1954; the second phase on March 30, 1954; and the third on May 1, 1954. Will the young artillerymen fighting for freedom, under relentless enemy bombing, with no tanks and no bombers, succeed against the superior French forces?

(**Editor's Note**: Text in italic and regular text between brackets have been provided by the Editor for context.)

Opposite: Detail, *Soldiers in the trenches,*
sketch, Điện Biên Phủ, 1954, graphite on
paper, 25 x 20.3cm. Collection of the artist.

The People's Army position their artillery in underground bunkers on mountain slopes surrounding the French fortress in Mường Thanh. General Giáp, in the first phase of the battle, prepares to launch a coordinated artillery and infantry attack[58] against the French strongholds of Him Lam[59] and Độc Lập.[60] Artillery Division 351 deploys all its regiments: Howitzer 105mm cannons, anti-aircraft guns 37mm,[61] mountain artillery 75mm pack Howitzers,[62] and 120mm mortars.[63]

March 11, 1954

Tâm spends his first night at the headquarters of Artillery Division 351, which is on a mountain top overlooking the French military fortress, located down below in the Mường Thanh Valley.

C805[64]

We unloaded ammunition from two vehicles four times in one night. There was only one tail-light. Dark.

At three o'clock in the morning, we began digging artillery bunkers for the 105mm artillery. Dig secretly, don't talk loudly ... Enemy cannons fired and exploded nine hundred feet away.

A truck going uphill rolled back ... the driver jumped out to save the truck, fell, injured, tried to prevent the truck from falling in the river. The company commander immediately praised his achievement.

On the road, we met up with the infantry:

"Hey! It's been a month since we've seen each other!"

One infantryman pleaded:

"Please let me touch the cannon."

Engineers and infantry built a shortcut through the jungle. The road ensures secrecy for artillery on the move. Bamboo and wooden frames with camouflage leaves ... difficult for enemy planes to spot our artillery.

March 12, 1954

At the headquarters of the artillery division.

In the newspaper: General Võ Nguyên Giáp calls for the destruction of all enemy troops at Điện Biên Phủ. Also a poem: "Hold onto to your Youth."[65] And a propaganda poster: "Determined to Win for Uncle Hồ!"

C757[66] shot and destroyed one Dakota and twelve planes at Điện Biên Phủ, receives a Third Class Victory Medal.

Two batteries won First Class Soldier Medals. One battery fired four shots and all four hit their targets. Another battery fired sixteen, and nine hit.

Officers and soldiers believe in: "Steady attack. Steady advance."

Some were impatient to fight without being prepared.

Two-thirds of the Army are satisfied with the guns and bunkers. Additional modifications will further improve living conditions ... Some soldiers lack a sense of protecting others.

Platoons take care of ammunition. There are cooks and nurses. We need more accommodation and underground depots for supplies.

Drivers worry about protecting their trucks. Some are afraid to leave them to get rice and dig fortifications.

Continuous marching, seven or eight days without a break, to get ammunition: climbing seven passes is still fun.

We stayed up through the night to prepare straw, thatch, and wood to build the underground artillery bunkers.

...

Crescent-moon night:

Enemy artillery fire from Mường Thanh[67] sparks waves of fire across the mountains.

I took time to rest in the underground bunker. The wind blew clumps of dirt onto my face. Soil falls all over my body. In the cramped tunnel, the stencil printing team keeps on working through the night to publish the newspaper of Artillery Division 351.

Earlier this afternoon, I climbed up a steep slope to the observation post. I'll get used to it. Looking down to the Điện Biên Valley, only fog and rising smoke. Here, three miles as the crow flies, we can monitor enemy artillery, aircraft, even infantry.

The observation team dug its own bunker, beautiful and sturdy; there are places to lie down covered with tarpaulin, stretched over a green bamboo frame, like in a boat. Pathet Lao books,[68] combat diaries ... the

walls are covered in canvas with timetables and maps. Comrade Tích watched and kept track of the enemy …

C757 just fired at three enemy "old lady" planes! The company received another Third Class Military Merit Medal.

"Uncle Hồ's letter has arrived!"[69]

Mr [Phạm Ngọc] Mậu,[70] the political commissar of the division, opened the letter and read it [standing] on top of the bunker:

"You are entering a battle.

I await reports of your achievements so I can commend the most prominent units and individuals.

I wish you big victories and embrace you."

March 13, 1954

At the headquarters of the artillery division. The artillery opens fire with 105mm Howitzer guns. Tâm reports live the coordinated attack.

4 p.m. Start firing

Comrade Thước, deputy commander of the regiment, received the order from the Command Headquarters to open fire.

"Fire at every plane!"

Conveying the words of the Commander-in-Chief [General Võ Nguyên Giáp] to the units that opened fire:

"This is a historic first battle. Comrades, shoot to hit and resolutely complete the mission!"

A company fired at targets in the East[71] … Comrade Trung Kiên (Battalion 954).[72]

"Hello! Bro Hồ Đệ, fire now, fire all! Both companies fire!"

Instruction passed by Comrade Hữu Mỹ, the regiment commander:

"Tell Hồ Đệ to fire the artillery guns and the 12.7mm machine guns immediately."

Opposite: Portrait, 1954, signed Huỳnh Biếc, Tâm's nom de guerre, graphite on paper, 15.2 x 10.2cm. Collection of the Ho Chi Minh City Fine Arts Museum.

L. [unidentified] turned around and smiled, honored to pass the first instruction to Hồ Đệ.

"Regiment commander Hữu Mỹ order to C803 to open fire!"

The entire regiment opens fire!![73]

Units reporting:

C803: Opened fire at 4:12 p.m.

C801: Opened fire at 4 p.m.

C802: Opened fire at 4:25 p.m.

Do Dục Kien, War Officer of the General Staff, reports the results to Hồng Lĩnh [code name of the General Command of the People's Army].

The southeast of the enemy airfield is on fire! Hit one plane, another took off.

C801 fired the opening salvo: the first shot hits a target! The third shot hits all the targets! Enemy artillery is out of action. Enemy vehicles can't move.

C802 fired two long-range shots, C803 fired the first fake long-range shot. The enemy fired back at the C802 fake battlefield (wooden cannons).[74]

C801: Hit eighty percent of our targets. Five shots hit the airfield.

C802: One-third of the shots hit their targets. Enemy artillery in the Central Zone is completely blocked and can't fire back.

Instructions

C801, C802, C803 fire continuously wherever enemy artillery appears!

C803 fires at enemy artillery on the airfield and controls the airfield!

Do not allow enemy aircraft to take off. Fire intensely. Fire shots of many ranges …

Battalion 1 report

There are eight fighter bombers and two "old ladies" on the enemy airfield.

Enemy artillery was discovered firing from a bunker in Mường Thanh, C803 counterattacked.

C803: Hit the enemy artillery battlefield at position 203, set fire to one warehouse (the unit fired fifty-three shells).

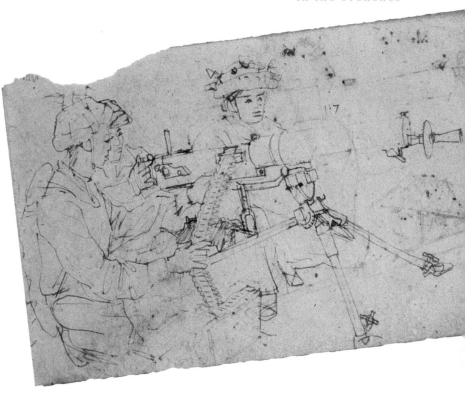

C801: Fire continuously.

C802: Fire 37mm anti-aircraft artillery guns.

Eight guns fired at the "old ladies" taking off in the south of the enemy airfield!

At Mường Thanh Airfield, vehicles tow fighter planes into shelters!

5:25 p.m.: A helicopter[75] landed in front of battlefield 307 (near the center of Mường Thanh).

Four enemy guns at position 201[76] fired where our infantry advanced.

Instructions

Our gunners fire at position 201 (at the foot of one of the D hills)[77] so

Above: Combatants, 1954, graphite on paper, 10.5 x 16cm. Collection of the Ho Chi Minh City Fine Arts Museum.

that our infantry can attack! Fire from the top to the foot of the hill!

Our infantry is thirteen hundred feet away from the enemy's barbed-wired fences. C801, C802 fire fiercely!

Nam Thắng, deputy political commissar of the regiment:

"All units, complete the mission. Unit firing at Hill D, intimidate the enemy and don't let them threaten our infantry!

"Enemy artillery is firing at the bridge where our infantry is advancing."

801 fired at enemy position 307 hitting the target; an "old lady" on the airfield was on fire. The division praised 801!

803 hit one hundred percent of the enemy battlefield in the north of the airfield, now shooting at the enemy airfield!

801 fired at enemy position 307a; no enemy artillery counterattacked?

802 fired at enemy position 307b.

803 fired two salvos of six shells, hitting a plane; and now firing at the second plane …

Hit one Dakota in the south of the airfield; the enemy plane is on fire!

Report

802: Hit Hill D.

Hit another "old lady" and one Dakota.

Firing at the southeast of the enemy airfield.

The division credited Battalion 954 and Comrade Trung Kiên!

Mậu, the political commissar, said:

"We must assist the infantry. All units must hit the targets!

"Fire at Mường Thanh until you hit!

"Enemy artillery in Mường Thanh is firing at Regiment 209 [a People's Army infantry regiment].[78] Our infantry hasn't gotten through yet! Regiment 141 already set explosives!"

Mậu again:

"We should comply with all infantry requirements, so that it's not a waste to pull guns in … Hello, is that you, Kiên? Remind all brothers not to be subjective[79] are you clear? The mission's not over until all

Opposite: Combatant, Điện Biên Phủ, 1954, ink on paper, 34 x 23cm. Collection of the Ho Chi Minh City Fine Arts Museum.

enemy stations are destroyed!

"The infantry got through one barbed-wire fence, they're asking the artillery to fire ...

"The infantry has set explosives and got through five fences!"

Three enemy stations were attacked.[80] We captured an officer from the enemy command. He tried to escape, but our soldiers struggled until he surrendered. A third-class enemy officer standing nearby said:

"If you surrender, I'll surrender!"

The infantry supported by the artillery was very confident: they damaged barbed-wire fences, moved in close, and attacked enemy areas 304, 306, and 303.

All stations on Him Lam were resolved at half past midnight![81]

We captured three hundred prisoners!

75mm mountain guns fired at eleven aircraft + F7 = thirteen aircraft.

Hương Thủy shot one "old lady," one fighter aircraft.

Our artillery fired continuously.

Instructions

Soldiers take time off to nap in situ so that when they receive orders to shoot, they can fire at once.

Some brothers showed hatred (*căm thù*)[82] and cried out in their sleep:

"Hit ... destroy the enemy!"

One gunner Number 1 woke up, sat up, grabbed the trigger cord, and shouted:

"Fire! Fire!"

Poem: "The French enemy in Điện Biên Phủ were afraid of our artillery."

March 14, 1954

At the headquarters of the artillery division. Tâm's friends from C804 are sent to seize an ammunition depot on the recently captured Him Lam.

Seize an enemy ammunition depot

Telegram from the high-level command of the division:

"Organize a Glory Team immediately to seize ammunition from an enemy depot."

Comrade Quang, the battalion officer, is in charge of about eighty people, including soldiers from C804, combat engineers, and security guards from the regiment.

Tough mission. Enemy artillery fired from position 6. Enemy guards were armed with handguns.

The team arrived at Him Lam. They stopped to observe. The enemy artillery was close.

One comrade said:

"It's going to be hard to go in!"

But the officers were determined:

"Go, even if the enemy fires at us!"

They walked crouching, and then ran fast for two and a half miles.

On Hill 2, they continued for more than a mile without trenches, through rows of barbed wire, active mines.

They kept going.

An enemy salvo targeted C804, with all types of guns … kicked up blinding dust, soil, rocks, fell on their backs.

Two officers ran up from the rear to encourage the men to keep calm. But the brothers were unable to move. They were worried:

"Lying here won't help."

They encouraged each other to follow the infantry spirit … determined to win.

At the second salvo, shrapnel fell on Quyết's back. He was injured but didn't scream. He tried to put a bandage on … found he was OK.

After the third enemy salvo, still nobody moved.

"Look, the ammunition is being carried out of the depot!"

The infantrymen had seized 105mm artillery shells.

More than two hundred enemy artillery shells came through!

"A taste of their own medicine!"

C804 comrades rushed to the ammunition depot to form a line.

Overleaf: Artillerymen and 105mm cannon in an underground bunker, Điện Biên Phủ, 1954, ink on paper, 20 x 27cm. Collection of the Ho Chi Minh City Fine Arts Museum.

Shells were quickly passed down the line.

Sappers who had gone to detonate mines were discovered.

Flares!

Big enemy planes flew in.

Three comrades were injured.

"Pass [the shells] to the end of the line."

"Spread the shells out! Don't slow down!"

Comrades Hòe, Huệ, Tâm came out last. Hill E.[83]

Hòe shouted:

"Hanh, two comrades [Huệ and Tâm] were killed! I'm injured ..."

"Where are the bodies [of Huệ and Tâm]?"

They needed eight comrades to carry the bodies.

Chèo was in there, not out yet.

Quyết encouraged his team to go back and get their comrades' bodies.

"We have team love and class love ... can you do it?"

Chèo led the brothers back. They ran crouching under exploding artillery shells.

"I've only found one comrade's body [Tâm]," Chèo reported.

Quyết decided to go back. He dug where the ground had collapsed and found Huệ's body ...

The brothers wrapped Huệ and Tâm in parachute cloth that they tied with ropes, and carried them back before dawn.

[Later,] Quyết returned to Him Lam to check on the ammunition. He reported to Hòe (who had been injured) and senior officers ... Over two hundred 105mm artillery shells!

"We've saved many ammunition trucks from traveling up here. Comrades sacrificed their lives to save our entire front a lot of blood; the enemy will pay the blood debt," Quyết said.

Our soldiers never laughed before while carrying heavy shells, running on bumpy, muddy paths, under enemy artillery [they were so happy to have seized so much ammo]! The gunners thanked the infantry ... The entire front thanked the infantry. The infantry had never felt more secure [thanks to the large supply of ammunition]: the artillery is the rhythm, the musical accompaniment for the infantry to attack.

March 15, 1954

At the headquarters of the artillery division, Tâm meets the young farmers recruited to operate secondhand 105mm cannons. They recount how, against all odds, they prevailed against superior French forces in the 1952 Hòa Bình Campaign.[84] *In 1953, C119 was renamed C806, and became part of Regiment 45.*[85] *At Điện Biên Phủ, the C806 guns were among the first to fire.*

Two 105mm Howitzer guns

C119 captured one gun in Thất Khê[86] from the French, and one in Đông Khê[87] during the 1950 Border Campaign. [They hid the guns.] The regiment took them out for drills in Cao Bằng.[88] The batteries were called up toward the end of the Hòa Bình Campaign on the second day of Tết (February 22, 1952).[89]

Artillery officers welcomed the new recruits. They all came from Cao Bằng and were very strong. The company marched [for over a hundred miles] to Thục Luyện[90] to welcome the two guns at Đoan Hùng.

There were four artillery platoons. Two guns. Two lots of ammunition. Only one platoon had guns. The squadron had no foundation. The camouflage on the barrel of one gun was attached to the clinometer (an instrument to measure firing and slope angles). It made the gun crooked. The *ni-vo* (the bubble level in the clinometer) was left open. They figured out how to use it. Luckily, it wasn't broken.

Comrade Tảo told his friends:

"We have two days to train the new recruits on how to use the guns … I'm very worried … they're all rookies."

Squadron officers became Number 1 and Number 8. Next day they practiced: finding firing ranges, adjusting the clinometer, finding elevation angles, testing, pushing, and pulling the guns …

The platoons without guns made preparations:

Braided ropes from jungle materials to haul the guns.

Made aiming posts from hollow trees.

Replaced bamboo with stronger bamboo below the gun carriages.

Made mats to camouflage the guns while moving them on the road.

On the afternoon of February 21, 1952, after the drills, the officers practiced and adjusted the guns until dark. The brothers finished eating

and began marching to their position, near Hòa Bình.

Order to complete the occupation later that night. The trucks arrived and towed the guns. After only three hundred feet, the trucks began skidding (*pa-ti-nê*). For two hours!

[One artilleryman recounted:]

"We were very worried we'd be late to the battlefield! We marched to Lạc Song [close to the battlefield]. Then we pulled the guns for a mile

Engineers repairing lines of communication,
1954, signed Huỳnh Biếc, graphite sketch on
paper, 10 x 14cm. Collection of the artist.

and a half. We used the engineers' large cables. They burned our hands. It was very painful. Ten new recruits hauled each gun. No shouting … only whispers … to keep our operation secret!

"By the time we hauled the guns from Route 41 to the battlefield, it was dawn.

"The battery needed two winches to pull the artillery uphill.

"At 11 a.m. on February 22, 1952, we reinforced fortifications, and completed occupation. But we were in such a rush, it was difficult to occupy the battlefield. Battery 2 didn't have enough oil, they couldn't fire … The telephone wires were broken.

"We finally opened fire at 7 a.m. on February 23, 1952.

"We received the order and loaded the shells.

"Five or six of the shells were smoke shells [used to hide movement from the enemy's line of sight]. We reported it to the political commissar:

—Smoke or whatever, fire them all! he shouted.

"We used leftover M3 ammunition for M2 guns.[91]

"The ground was so hard we couldn't hammer the tips of the aiming posts into the ground … We had to dig to bury them!

"The trigger cord of the first gun didn't work—we tied it to the handle to fire! After the first shot, the gun was in order again. We were worried we didn't have enough oil and that the gun wouldn't fire! But both guns fired well.

"We asked Regiment 675 for a topographical survey. It was difficult terrain. The artillerymen cleared reeds to measure every hundred feet.

"We didn't have the standard aiming posts we needed—we had to make bamboo cross sticks.

"At 7 a.m., order to open fire. We finished the survey and had the elevation angles at 6:50 a.m. … the right data for the guns to adjust their sights. One gun was at the top of the hill. The other gun was at the bottom. A single commander couldn't command the entire company!

"Battery 1 test-fired.

"Battery 2 opened fire. The first shot hit an enemy bunker! Immediate commendation from Command Headquarters.

"In the first battle, both guns fired and hit their targets. Some shots hit the enemy artillery, but the enemy quickly withdrew.

"Whenever we fired, enemy soldiers jumped into their tunnels. When we stopped firing, they jumped back out and retreated.

"The enemy was confused and called for help from Hanoi … Enemy planes flew in to bomb us. Our gunners stayed calm, kept firing. The bombs didn't directly hit our battlefield … camouflage leaves flew in all directions …

"At 1 p.m. on February 22 [1953], we targeted the Ngọc Pier to block enemy withdrawal to Hòa Bình. Taking range from the map, we hit the main road. Our infantry cheered. The enemy thought our infantry was attacking them, so they dispersed and ran.[92]

"[After the battle at the Ngọc Pier,] breakfast was brought early, but we were so busy … we didn't eat until 3 p.m. There was a shortage of rice. Only six ounces a day. The cook bought cassava in remote villages, and mixed it in with boiled rice and pickled leeks. A delicious Hòa Bình dish! Faces were dirty … but happy.

"Two batteries were recorded on the division Golden Exploit Board.

"The afternoon of the following day, we hid the guns in reeds, and withdrew to Thục Luyện District [a sixteen-hour march] and prepared to attack La Phù [in the French-occupied zone].

As we left the battlefield, we unexpectedly met General Võ Nguyên Giáp. The General allowed a shot against a bunker at the Ba Vành post [a former fortified French camp]to test demolition capability.[93] Gun number two fired well!

"We were ordered to withdraw and regroup to attack La Phù. We hid the artillery and assigned a unit to guard it. Most of the soldiers were merged into the 12.7mm unit temporarily.

"We returned to Phú Thọ[94] to cut off the enemy's reserve force. [After the French army withdrew from Phú Thọ,] the unit moved to Yên Bái to welcome Regiment 45. We officially merged with the first 105mm artillery regiment of Vietnam! We were all happy that our unit would now be stronger!"

That was April 1953. Battery 3: Quý, Thòng, Kim, Thuyết.

Battery 4: Mịch, Tương, Điểm, Lânđ, Văn.

Platoon officers: Doanh and Tuệ …

Here at Điện Biên, the two historic guns fought as part of the large formation of artillery regiments and brigades. They coordinated with anti-aircraft defense guns, mountain guns, engineers, and the infantry. C806 fired the first salvo at Him Lam, opening the historic Điện Biên Phủ Campaign.

In the Điện Biên Campaign, C806 hit the following targets:

Seven shots hit loopholes, demolished four enemy bunkers. Hit one "old lady," three Dakota planes, one jeep. Hit the enemy's lead gun.

Cut off enemy troops reinforcing Độc Lập Hill, withdrawing troops from Bản Kéo [the French stronghold Anne-Marie] and paratroopers. Many enemy died ...

Took control of the enemy artillery positions in the southeast of the airfield during the Battle of Him Lam.

Infantry and civic workers cheered the artillery as they marched.

"Silence! Keep quiet! Do you want us to be discovered?" an old civic worker asked.

"Roar well!" he added.

And he gave the cannon nozzle an affectionate pat.

Slogan written on the shield of a cannon in one of the artillery bunkers of Battery 3, C119 (now C806):

"Victory in Hòa Bình on March 22, 1952, certain victory again in Trần–Đình!" (alias Điện Biên Phủ). The motto reflects the tradition of the artillery of the Việt Nam People's Army.

March 16, 1954

At the headquarters of the artillery division, C805 artillerymen remember their comrades who were killed while hauling the cannons to Điện Biên Phủ up and down steep hills. During the first phase of the battle, they suffered additional losses when they attacked Hồng Cúm,[95] an enemy stronghold five miles to the south of the French headquarters.

Overleaf: Caring for a wounded soldier,
Điện Biên Phủ, 1954, ink on paper,
10.5 x 16cm. Collection of the artist.

An example in struggle

C805 artillerymen were hauling the guns up the Lũng Lô Pass. They cut down a tree and wedged it near the gun's oil pipe. Trần Văn Ngưu, the squad deputy leader, afraid the gun would slide down the hill, stepped in to support it ... the cannon suddenly crushed his hip and leg. Terrible pain. But he didn't scream. He didn't want the gun-carriage driver to panic so close to a precipice ... He was given emergency care ... he thought of his parents who were killed by the enemy.

"Dear comrades, please fight to avenge me," he said.

Mậu replaced Ngưu.

On a slope "using seven winches," a gun thundered downhill. Mậu, afraid that tree branches would break the sight device, rushed to try to stop it. His legs were crushed ... it took a long time for his comrades to pull him out from under the wheel. Bạt, the political instructor, kept encouraging them. He was freed by evening and finally out of danger. Mậu went back to fight a few days later.

Comrade Trúc wedged his shoulders under the gun to keep it from falling into the ravine. He was killed ... Tô Vĩnh Diện was killed crushed by a cannon ... and Phan Đình Giót was killed when he blocked a damaged loophole with his body during the attack on Him Lam!

In Điện Biên, the C805 artillerymen fought against eight enemy guns in Hồng Cúm. [During the battle,] enemy planes destroyed the fortifications with napalm bombs. Many different types of bombs fell around the fortifications. The enemy used smoke bombs to protect their aircraft when bombing.

A captured enemy officer admitted:

"After we were hit by your shots, we had only one cannon left," while the C805 guns were safe.

Topographical soldiers found emplacements on peaks, some covered in jungle, others bare. They set up twenty-nine observation posts. They dug artillery bunkers day and night. They ate once a day. On top of the hills, there was no water to wash. They went to sleep covered in dust and soil ...

There are bunkers for the performance troops and over two hundred safe underground shelters to hide in during bombing raids.

Topographical engineer: Việt ... Information soldiers: Cự, Phụng, Toản.

Phụng was buried under the rubble during a bombing raid. He dug himself out and restored communication. Việt was on watch when he was hit by an explosion, tried to get up ...

Every night, the infantry squadron walked to the jungle, chopped trees, and carried back logs to reinforce the artillery bunkers.

Bombs burned the telephone lines ... Toản jumped out of the trenches to fix the line. Fumbling around, he touched a burning shell fragment. He remembered that Trụ had been killed holding a telephone line ...

Comrades Bảng and Giảng were killed. A bomb hit their shelter and it collapsed...They were holding onto the receivers, earphones on, when they were found ...

Enemy artillery fire and bombing raids were so fierce that the soldiers hid in covered shelters. But the engineers went out into the open to reconnect damaged communication lines, even without instructions or encouragement from their officers.

The success of the People's Army's coordinated artillery and infantry assault on March 13 took the French by surprise. Before the attack, Charles Piroth, the commander of the French artillery force at Điện Biên Phủ,[96] had reassured De Castries: "No Viet cannon will fire more than three rounds before it is located and destroyed." Two days later, on March 15, Piroth, deeply depressed by the failure of the French artillery, apologized to his fellow officers, returned to his bunker, and removed the pin from a grenade.

March 17, 1954
At the headquarters of the division artillery: Keeping up morale, enjoying a performance between two cannons, joking about "rice full of cockroach shit," and mourning the loss of comrades and friends. Tâm alludes to his crush for the singer Ms Tý. When he got in touch with her after the war, he discovered she had married Kính, the company commander mentioned in the diary.

The squadron leader was listening to the radio transmission. The men continued chatting, some leaned on gun shields and wheels, others discussed Soviet and Chinese paintings.

Suddenly, the order came:

"Prepare to fire at the enemy infantry!"

The fuse detonated immediately toward firing position 303, shells loaded ...

Motto on the shield:

"Victory in Hòa Bình, March 22, 1952, definite victory in Trần–Đình!"

The soldiers call the "old lady" an evil landowner. The other day, "old lady" planes dropped smoke bombs near our battlefield ... One "old lady" flew over and was shot several times by our anti-aircraft 37mm guns and chased away ...

A Grumman F6F Hellcat caught fire, broke into pieces and fell like a kite with a broken string ... the battlefield resounded with cheers.

Mr Tuyên Kính, the battalion political commissar, is a respected teacher. He appears neat, straightforward, and deliberate. He went to the artillery bunker to play chess with the brothers. Such normal behavior during combat makes the soldiers feel calm ...

News from Command Headquarters: three companies of French and puppet soldiers surrendered in Bản Kéo.[97]

The entertainers of Artillery Division 351 ... Minh Tiến, Tụy Lanh, Vinh Lương, Tý, Ngọc ... held a performance in the artillery bunker ... with singing and dancing ... the stage was between two cannons ...

Everyone was there except the company commander Kính who was at the observation post, a mile and a half away ...

After being introduced to Kính by phone, Ms Tý said:

"You don't have to come to the bunker, just listen over the receiver!"

She sang *Xẩm Xoan* [a folk love song] through the receiver:

"The rice ripens ... Ah the rice is heavy with grains *i ì i* ..."

At the end of the song, she said:

"The report is over! ..."

Other soldiers told me: Company Commander Kính kept observing the enemy station, while listening to Ms Tý singing through the phone, regularly saying, "uhm uhm …" as if he was listening to a report.

At times I joined in to sing and recite poems like this one by Tố Hữu[98]:

"What a joy this morning in May
On the way to the Việt Bắc to visit Uncle Hồ …"

❦

We eat water spinach, wild water celery, wild forest greens, wild banana flower; sometimes we have buffalo meat, sesame, and salt (roasted and crushed) … with "tiny sticky rice." The rice is stored in warehouses in the Northwest and brought here by pack bicycles from the rear in rain and sun … it's mixed with dry grains and cockroach shit, has a musty smell, and is as tasteless as pasty sticky rice … It's delicious!

Comrade Tràng, C806 "foster brother," brought the rice up the hill from the kitchen down in the ravine to congratulate his unit.

"I heard the news … our artillery shots were very good," he announced, out of breath.

Mr Kiên told me the story of the battle [against the French strongholds, Him Lam and Độc Lập]:

"An enemy jeep exploded. Enemy troops reinforcing Độc Lập ran wild and retreated to the airfield, pursued by our artillery … the enemy deserved such a counterattack after firing at our infantry!

"Him Lam was the first to be destroyed. The soil on the hill was charred by shelling. The airfield was littered with the wreckage of 'old lady' planes and white parachutes, color of mourning.

"A Dakota that landed was targeted by our artillery, and quickly took off again.

"Red Cross ambulance workers couldn't pick up a body. It was wrapped in a French flag. Probably a high-ranking officer."

I met Thủ, the leader of a topographic platoon. Thủ has a short beard and is fond of composing lyrics:

… Oh topographic guy,
You look at the distant sky
And smile …

C804 deputy political commissar Khu called to report:

"Hey, we're watching the singers' performance…"

Meanwhile, our shells hit the airfield.

When the artillerymen receive instructions, the performers stop singing, gunners load shells, and wait for the order to fire.

Đình Tịnh wrote a satirical poem and pasted it on the wall of the artillery bunker:

Enemy posts are brightly lit in Điện Biên

Our shots black out their lights

Their officers and soldiers crawl into holes.

They dare not poke their heads out.

I met up with Mong, a gunner with Battery 2, formerly with Battery 1:

Mong was back from a rescue mission. A truck loaded with artillery shells overturned and fell into a precipice … My friends Phây and Duyên were in the truck, sitting on ammunition boxes. They were crushed by the boxes and killed! I loved them very much.

I'm distressed and sad.

They were so young, honest, and innocent.

I'm twenty-two years old and a political instructor and reporter. I'm not in charge of a specific unit. But I've been to many units and know many soldiers … I have the same feelings as an officer who is sad at losing brothers from his unit.

My friend Lê Thi, too, he volunteered for a mission during an operation, and his thigh was crushed by a cannon …

Several of us were also killed when a time-bomb exploded during the regiment's march to the front.

The first time we saw our comrades killed, many of us, officers and soldiers, cried … Then the second time, the third, it was as if our tears had been swallowed inside, giving way to action, to fight the enemy.

Mong reflected:

"During training, pulling artillery uphill was very difficult when we were in rough places … But the slopes of the training ground were nothing compared to the battlefield!

"Is this the challenge of life and death, the revolutionary spirit, when hatred is mixed with the determination to win? … Slopes are steep, sixty-five degrees! The heavy artillery gun weighs two tons. When the ropes break, there's nothing to hold it back … the gun plunges into the abyss … Brothers who can't get out of the way in time are crushed.

"The enemy artillery also kills us, but our troops continue to advance.

"Enemy soldiers will pay for their crimes!"

Opposite: Officers standing on the battlefield, Điện Biên Phủ, 1954, sketch, graphite on paper, 27 x 20cm. Collection of the Ho Chi Minh City Fine Arts Museum.

The battalion command asked Hồ and Thanh from the diversion team to find out individuals' names to reward them:

"I'll try!"

The artillery diversion teams have courage and deserve awards.

They create fake artillery emplacements with fake barrels made of wood … installed in secret places …

Smoke from real artillery explosions conceal the fakes … the gunners [from the fake guns] quickly retreat to ready-made trenches … enemy artillery counterattack and pound the fake battlefield, while the real artillery is kept secret and safe. It's a very dangerous game for our soldiers.

The enemy can't play this game … even though the French artillery is strong, scientifically positioned on the battlefield, well known for its "professionalism," and has a lot of ammunition, they're positioned in the valley and we surround them on the hillsides.

* * *

The men in Battery 3 had just finished eating when the performance artists returned from their visit to the observation post.

The singers Ms Minh, Ms Tý, said:

"Today we saw with our own eyes the shells you fired at the enemy … so beautiful!"

—So you really saw bullets? Commander Kính asked.

Ms Minh and Ms Tý replied with songbird voices:

"Yes, we saw an enemy plane and their infantry running away!"

Loud laughter.

The gunners joked around and spoke to them with affection as they would to their younger sisters.

"Did you like it …? Such an unforgettable event, isn't it …?"

Laughter echoed in the underground bunker.

Even Comrade Độ, the platoon officer who rarely spoke, smiled.

In the evening, we were given sugar and tobacco … It wasn't much, but it was fun, contributing to the party between the two cannons in the bunker.

We're steadily surrounding the enemy! Enemy planes have stopped dive-bombing ... They drop their bombs from high up in the sky.

Our infantry continues to dig trenches day and night, directing their "spears" toward Mường Thanh.

March 18, 1954

At the headquarters of the artillery division, Tâm inquires about artillery and infantry coordination during the attack against Him Lam.

I asked Phượng about the battle against Him Lam:

"We were two small hills away from the enemy, within firing range of a rifle. At 3 a.m. we tried firing. The infantry started advancing in secret. Our artillery fire hit all the hills. We didn't miss.

"We coordinated with the infantry. The artillery fired from above, the infantry used explosive charges from below.

"We demolished a bunker and captured three enemy soldiers.

"We captured Kinh and Thái soldiers fighting for the enemy. They were touched by how well we treated them.

"One of our infantryman said:

—I long to fire just one shot ... after that I'll die satisfied ...

"And, after we adjusted our firing range, those infantrymen jumped out of the trenches, smiling as they attacked.

"Our guns demolished the French flagpole! A comrade rushed to plant Uncle Hồ's flag on top of Him Lam! He saw an officer decapitated.

"The regiment commander had told the infantryman Phụng to carry a two-way radio transmitter with him.

—Request guns to fire fiercely in four minutes, Phụng asked.

"Phụng's attack order was heard loud and clear!

—Move forward!

"Him Lam fortress had been praised as an [impregnable] fortress by Navarre,[99] Cogny,[100] Nguyễn Văn Tâm,[101] and the American Advisor.[102]"

Phong, the political instructor in charge of performance troops with Artillery Division 351, Brother Viện, a middle-aged Party member[103] who was very keen on traditional music, and Phạm Vinh, another Party member, wrote combat lyrics to the tune of a traditional folk song (*Xẩm Xoan*):

The artillery fires at enemy bunkers
Row after row of their bunkers are destroyed
Day and night the guns roar—the enemy is terrified.
We fight hard, to overcome difficulties
Tan tính tình … tính tang
Overcome the endless struggle
Determined to overcome
The people are waiting, waiting for victory.
The people together raise productivity.
The enemy must die.
This time our artillery swears … we will destroy the enemy.
Tang tính tình tình … Tình tính tang tang …

March 19, 1954
At the headquarters of the artillery division.

Dạ, the company political officer, read the names of comrades praised by the regiment and awarded certificates of merit. Then he read the names of officers punished for breaking the "five battlefield disciplines."

Khả, the nurse, reported on the medical situation … he received many favorable comments from colleagues.

We've learned lessons from the first phase, and are preparing for the second and third phases.

Some brothers were impatient to attack immediately, but we first had to strengthen our artillery bunkers.

Opposite: Caring for a wounded soldier, Điện Biên Phủ, 1954, ink on paper, 10.5 x 16cm. Collection of the artist.

Between March 20 and March 30, the campaign enters its second phase. The artillery is ordered to move the heavy guns closer to the French positions and build new fortifications. The infantry expands the network of trenches toward the French strongholds fortified with deep barrages of barbed wire and minefields. Will the second attack succeed in overrunning the next line of French strongholds?

March 20, 1954

At the headquarters of the artillery division (or perhaps on a hill nearby occupied by C804 after Him Lam was captured).

C804 was hit. The bunker collapsed.

Tý, Lộc, and Giao were killed.

Ngọ from Battery 2 was wounded.

The battalion launched a "hate the enemy" campaign.

We have entered a new phase of attack. We are leaving our current fortifications.

March 21, 1954

At the headquarters of the artillery division. Tâm and the C804 artillerymen prepare under the cover of darkness to transport the 105mm Howitzers to a new position to attack the French fortress on Hill D.

Our three comrades in Battery 2 were killed. Immediately replaced. Hùng, the new captain and deputy platoon officer, has experience in combat (Regiment 675), activities, and thought-management.

Engineers work from noon to night to repair the gun. The fork was rusted, slightly flattened, and caked in mud, but still functions ... (taken from the Battle of Đoan Hùng–Việt Bắc in 1950).

"Just use it temporarily ... we'll exchange it for a new one from Mường Thanh," the engineers said.

In the evening, I joined the Artillery Division 351 performance troops for a party with the artillerymen from Battery 2.

We recited propaganda poems to encourage hatred ...

Order to leave at 1 a.m.!

I got up in the dark, and rustled together my canvas blanket and backpack.

I heard the battery commander Kiều Văn Xích say:

"Open the tunnel door, bring the artillery out."

The gunners first carried out ammunition, stakes, mallets, bamboo bundles, chocks, spare-parts boxes, and other miscellaneous parts.

Cooperation: infantrymen and AA gunners came to help, and over twenty soldiers hauled out the gun ...

The silhouettes of the soldiers were etched on the skyline above the Điện Biên Valley. Clouds and mist cleared from halfway up the mountain down to the fields below. Flares flickered brightly, then faded ...

The voice of the battery commander Xích:

"Two, three, two, three ..."

Everyone struggled to pull, push, force the gun carriages to the right, left, chock quickly ... Then again, "heave-ho," downhill.

The winch made a loud noise.

Near the bottom of the slope, the gun accelerated down the hill, pulling everyone along with it ... Artilleryman Number 4 was lucky ... he jumped quickly out of the way, pressed the gun carriage into the ground, avoided being crushed ... the cannon came to a sudden halt!

After his escape, the infantrymen joked:

"I see my Vietnamese comrades are suffering ... No less, maybe even more than at the Battle of Stalingrad.[104]"

After the gun carriages were reassembled, ten *Mô-lô-tô-va*[105] trucks towed the guns away as quickly as a cat snatches a mouse.

We arrived at Suối Reo ...

We all gathered to push the artillery into bunkers. We hid the shells, camouflaged the guns, and cut bamboo ...

Night operation

[The following night.]

Company operation on the road at night, no one can see a thing. Rụ, the political commissar, reminds us to overcome difficulties. Then we waited for the moon to rise and took advantage to get some sleep.

Facsimile of the diary pages dated
March 31 and April 1, 1954, 22 x 28cm.
Collection of the Điện Biên Phủ Museum.

At 1 a.m. we got up, ready to carry ammunition—on foot because the trucks transported the artillery and other heavy loads.

The drivers strained their eyes to see ... two led the way, holding up a piece of white cloth, one on each side of the road.

The truck broke down (*pan/en panne*). Long wait, cold.

Another chance to get some "sleep": standing up to sleep, sitting down to sleep, hugging a cannon to sleep.

Deputy Company Captain Thắng paced back and forth, worried: some trucks were ahead, but one was stuck near a stream ...

Order to camouflage. Then we pushed, pulled the truck uphill.

Moon of the nineteenth Lunar day. The trucks towing the artillery ran fast through the fields. Enemy planes flew during the night because they feared our anti-aircraft guns during the day. Their planes were loud, our trucks too. Three more miles to reach the main road: infantrymen hung their mosquito nets and slept right there, by the side of the track.

On a muddy, rutted slope, a truck broke down again ... Again blocking, pulling, carrying wood to secure the road ... The truck screeched, moving backward and forward several times. When we got through, it was dawn.

Tonight is two nights and a day without sleep. Our soldiers are tired but happy. In the morning, they unloaded shells, bullets, dug fortifications, camouflaged trucks, ate, and slept.

Sudden order:

Everyone build fortifications for five days except the battery commander and gunners Numbers 1 and 8.

The General's words:

"We are determined to use our energy to build our battlefield firmly. We know that the more we work and sweat, the less we bleed ..."

March 24, 1954
At a rest stop near Route 41, on the way to the new C804 fighting position.

Learned from the General's letter:

Build an attack-and-siege battlefield!

Our soldiers are too subjective, complacent: they stand on top of their

bunkers and cheer whenever an enemy plane falls and Him Lam is on fire.
Guideline: "Fight firmly, advance firmly."
"Steady attack, steady advance."
Combined with:
Land Reform.[106]
The Geneva Conference (Five Powers).[107]

\ι̣

Report from the officers' meeting:
There is anxiety but the brothers continue to build fortifications.
Platoon 2 is worried that the artillery guns are too close to the road...
the company replied that 12.7mm heavy machine gun units have been
called up to the hilltop.
Brother Xuân Thành is having mood swings, especially since the
singers' performance. He seems homesick, absent-minded, not doing
much work ... He's a student from a middle-class family, so it's natural
for him to be different from those who come from poor peasant families.
It's normal. In these difficult and fiercely stressful times, the fleeting
sight of "pink shadows," and female beauty makes us feel happy and
full of yearning ...
A *petit bourgeois* emotion—isn't it?

\ι̣

The trucks arrived early morning. Tuy and Tý his co-driver said it had
been difficult driving during the night. Narrow roads, deep ravines, and
very dark. They drove as if rowing a boat in a dream ... One side of their
truck was flattened ... but better than falling into the void!
"Enemy bombs and cannons are nothing. Our own sacrifice is nothing.
Our biggest worry is the trucks falling off a cliff, the people's property
entrusted to us, destroyed."
I'll remember Ngọ forever. [Ngọ was wounded three days before.] He
had serious injuries—his hand, head, and chest. He needed surgery but
he said to the doctor he didn't want any anesthetic ... he told stories
about the battle.

"Did I lose a rib? ... Yes, you can lie, I wouldn't complain!" he joked, after the operation.

We have entered a new phase in the campaign, we are moving toward the center, leaving our fortifications behind.

March 27, 1954
Tâm and the C804 artillerymen are on the move again. Following the trucks towing the 105mm guns, they traverse a landscape on fire.

Night of march and siege
The company commander shouted:
"Order: Two batteries, march!"
"Order: All four batteries, march now! Hurry up!"
In the afternoon, the enemy dropped napalm. This evening, fires blazed on one side of the jungle. Heavy fog, stark dark sky. Enemy planes dropped fire bombs. The planes circled in the sky but below the trucks kept moving. How dare they threaten our spirit!
The bridges were bombed!
The engineers repaired them.
"Ah, 105mm guns! Go and beat them up! Shoot 'em up motherfuckers!"
Tế, a gunner, followed a truck, arms around the gun barrel ... even on sharp bends and turns. Watching the flickering lights of fire bombs, Tế hugged the barrel with affection ... he's also a very nice person.
The trucks suddenly stopped.
[We had arrived at our new position.]
Today it seemed so easy to occupy the battlefield, a walk in the park. Everyone was subjective and complacent.
[We're by] the large stream that flows into Điện Biên. Red fires on burnt hills. Sounds of machine guns. Enemy artillery fired then fell silent. They often target this road.

Opposite: Soldiers carrying ammunition through the trenches, graphite sketch on paper, 25 x 20cm. Collection of the artist.

Carrying M3 submachine guns and ammunition made in China ...

Tý and Sang, the truck drivers, said goodbye.

"We're going to hide the trucks! Good luck hitting your targets and shooting down their headquarters!" they said, shaking hands.

"Sure. You're the legs of the artillery, so please be ready too!" Thanh, Number 8, replied.

Great cooperation between drivers and gunners.

I fell asleep; Quý, the platoon leader, woke me up:

"Wake up, men! Hurry up! Go help carry artillery Number 4, the truck has broken down near the river!"

At night, the enemy fired mortars to destroy our fortifications.

In the early morning, nearby hills were scorched by napalm bombs. The company deputy commander instructed us to camouflage.

We all disguised ourselves.

Engineers Thanh and Phiến calculated direction and distance.

We're a mile and a half from Hill D, and two and a half miles from Mường Thanh.

We've received woven handkerchiefs embroidered with floral ethnic patterns in cheerful colors:

"I'm from Chi Luông, to the front-line soldier I'm waiting for ..."

"We're waiting ..." from the women in Pá Ham hamlet.

March 28, 1954

At the C804 new command post, ready to attack Hill D.

Letter from the General:

"Officers and soldiers must have the same determination as the leaders. Be determined to fight bravely, move and demolish fast, attack as strongly as the wind, take every chance to kill the enemy ... Move up to replace the fallen at the front. Officers and Party members must set the example for the entire Army. Each and every soldier will be an example going forward to kill enemies. Keep up the momentum. Do not fear difficulties. Do not fear injury. Let the enemy be terrified by our sight. Everyone must show determination. Compete to raise the fight-and-win flag of President Hồ!"

March 29, 1954
*At the C804 new command post, ready to attack the French stronghold on
Hill D.*

In the bunker
A smell of gunpowder and wet earth, ardent but deeply fragrant. I keep
banging my head on the roof of the tunnel: soil falls on my head, down
my neck, sticks in my hair.

Last night, soldiers delivered more munitions, slept for a few hours,
and left again at dawn.

The observation post reported:

"The forecast is for rain and showers ... enemy fighter planes aren't
taking off! ..."

We took advantage to prepare elevation angles, cut down trees, dig
holes for latrines, bathing areas ...

The enemy is probably worried they're living in a hollow place!

Sound of running echoes through our bunkers ... News from our new
anti-aircraft defense force: they've occupied the battlefield near the
enemy airfield!

Through the artillery sight device
Hill D, Mường Thanh Valley—two and a half miles away—and Him
Lam are all clearly visible. Tuất had a good laugh watching enemy
soldiers running to evade our artillery fire.

The enemy were building new fortifications. Whirlwinds of dust. Guys
ran back and forth, crept in and out, hunched over to get into the
trenches, huddling in holes ... like crabs and fiddler crabs ...

[I can see] the mountains on the Laotian side. At night, fog whitens
the fields in the Điện Biên Valley. A funeral veil covered enemy posts
and villages nearby. The Nậm Rốm River[108] flows through Mường Thanh.
Beautiful day expected tomorrow ... clear observation ... O artillery,
our advancing infantry are close to enemy fences!

121

The General's letter:

"Determined to present victory to the Party and Uncle Hồ—cooperate with battlefield Number 5, Zone V, and the South … Celebrate the success of the Land Reform and spread the good news to the peace-loving people of the world!"

❧

Mr Nam Thắng [briefed us ahead of our attack against Hill D]:

"We've set up new artillery commands. It's possible that we'll develop new armed units to attack, capture enemy guns, and then use their emplacements as our own …

"Prepare to fight non-stop, but keep a normal daily routine: eat, drink sleep, wash … and a good water supply for the artillery.

"The enemy in Điện Biên faces a shortage of wood. They're collecting wood from parachuted drops and surrounding trenches.

"Our infantry is digging trenches closer and closer to the enemy, reaching across the main road from Mường Thanh to Hồng Cúm, linked with enemy trenches (like an iron hand reaching to strangle the enemy).

"Uncle Hồ and Comrade Trường Chinh[109] are looking forward to combat news from our Regiment 45 … We are determined to plant Uncle's flag on top of Hill D![110]"

❧

Đình Tịnh, an information soldier, wrote in his notebook:

"We are the blood of our company,

We spill our blood so the people can live.

Aha, we are the four brothers: Lưu, Huỳnh, Lộc, Tịnh …"

He's pinned up newspaper clippings of smiling Chinese children on the bunker wall, a cypher to decrypt Morse code … and a "poem" he composed to help him remember the Morse code.

Opposite: Artillerymen manning an anti-aircraft cannon,
Điện Biên Phủ, 1954, sketch, ink on paper, 15 x 20cm.
Collection of the artist.

The second phase of the battle is expected to start on March 30 with a coordinated artillery barrage and infantry attacks against the French fortified strongholds on Hills D, E, C, and A.

March 30, 1954
At the C804 new command post, on a mountain slope facing Hill D.

Before the H-Hour
Officers and soldiers' spirit is like the tree in front of our bunker.

The initial call to prepare to fire is set for 1 p.m.

Two engineers arrived to chop down a tree …

It's raining … the tree trunk is as wide as a circle of six people standing at arm's length from each other … Anti-aircraft gunmen, iron helmets on their heads, pass by, encourage the engineers.

They compliment "the nice guys in green clothes who patiently chop and saw down trees!"

Close to the start time to open fire, the tree cracks and falls: "Boom" ... Hurrah! Everyone cheered!

Work done, engineers crawled into the artillery bunker.

"Adjust fire!"

The artillery captain said:

"Uncle Hồ's flag is here, with your contribution and many medals—to mark the first shot of the battle."

5 p.m. Order to fire seven shots ... continuous booms toward the enemy ...

"Mường Thanh is on fire!"

"Turn right 3, elevation angle 235, two shots, fire!"

"Battery 1 hit the top of Hill D. Excellent!"

"Hit an enemy bunker! Hurray!"

Tê's voice:

"Fight to avenge Tý, Giao, Lộc [killed on March 20]!"

Shooting on Hill D and two Thái battalions at 201 ... The enemy continue to surrender.

The trigger puller is bent.

Call the repairers now!

Shells blocked ... Unblock immediately!

The fight-to-win flag is hung in our headquarters.

Quý smiles:

"C804 succeeded in its mission to destroy enemy posts as ordered. Enemies who attacked us on this side are hurrying back to the other side of the Nậm Rốm River.

"We are sniping and isolating them in small groups ... On the north hills of the airfield ... enemy planes dropped aid packages ..."

March 31, 1954
At the C804 command post facing Hill D. Three C804 artillerymen were injured during the attack against Hill D.

A bomb exploded at the entrance of the shelter of Battery 4 exactly when our artillery fired. The twin blasts were so powerful, shrapnel flew into the underground chamber. The wheels and range finder of the cannon were damaged. Châu, Number 7, was checking warheads. He felt a burning pain, looked down, and saw blood ... Lộc, Number 8, and Cường, Number 2, were also hurt. They were in pain but remained calm. Châu checked their injuries, called for treatment, then checked the guns.

The combat logbook was torn by shell fragments ...

"Keep it like that, and continue writing ... it gives it more meaning!" said Tuấn.

After he was injured, Lộc handed over to Độ and told him to be careful. He promised to be back when his wound was better.

"I'll stay, I'm not badly injured," Châu said.

News
Seven hills were resolved, and Uncle's flag is flying!
Enemy counterattacked Hill D.

April 1, 1954
Tâm leaves the C804 command post through trenches to go to Hill D where an enemy counterattack has been underway.

Take enemy ammunition to shoot them!
I heard that the infantry called for more ammunition. They seized three enemy 105mm guns and an ammunition depot!

Artillerymen, except Numbers 1, 7, 8, from Platoon 3 followed the company political deputy to Hill D.

[I followed them to Hill D through the trenches.]

Fields were ploughed with bomb craters, shells everywhere.

Him Lam was somber, bare, and bloody. The infantry has dug trenches to within ten feet of the enemy barbed-wire fences ... squelched in mud ...

I met the infantrymen as they were coming down Hill D. They carried spoils of war, ammunition, guns, 81mm mortars, artillery shells, maps ... they stopped for food at the vaulted entrance of a trench. Rice balls wrapped in banana leaves. Clothes and guns were muddy. Exhausted,

Battery 4 playing cards, April 16, 1954 (Khau doi 4, Tu-lo-khe), ink on paper, 20.3 x 17.8cm. Collection of the Ho Chi Minh City Fine Arts Museum.

the soldiers slept, hands covering their faces, toes poking out of rubber sandals, full of mud …

Two comrades fell asleep, their arms around each other's shoulders. They shared a tiny space at the vaulted entrance of a trench.

The cook, over thirty, kind-hearted, had brought two loads of rice and boiled water for soldiers and officers from his unit … he couldn't keep the grit out … It didn't matter. Just drink the water with the sweat, labor, and love of the cook who has chosen to serve our units … No wonder we call the cooks "foster brothers."

The ammunition and guns taken from the enemy were brand-new.

A young soldier was covered in mud, but smelt of perfume he had taken from an enemy parachute!

The wounded on stretchers … Blood …

Two enemy soldiers who had surrendered had only one rice ball between them. The guy holding the whole rice ball kept it for himself.

"Well, this guy is sick," he said.

\\ξ

The enemy mounted a counterattack against Hill D. Seemed bitter and vengeful. But our infantry blocked them. The enemy ran.

Brigades 304 and 316 called to praise our artillery units!

The newly created artillery company was called up … They received orders to wait in the trenches, follow the infantry advance, wait for the infantry to capture the enemy cannons, and then counterattack immediately using the enemy guns!

Infantrymen back from the enemy posts carried grenades, magazines, hand grenades … rifles, submachine guns. Some were carrying 105mm ammunition on their shoulders.

"Are you artillerymen? Cool!"

"Yes!" we all shouted in reply.

They passed the ammunition down the trench from shoulder to shoulder, boisterous and good-humored.

"Goodbye, fire accurately! Here, take this shell, aim it at Navarre's command post, so we can move in and attack," they said.

The infantrymen went back up the hill for more enemy ammunition.

"Keep going, brothers! We'll bring more down," they said.

We held onto the shell they gave us, moved by the solidarity between infantry and artillerymen!

Infantrymen nearby were cleaning enemy guns.

"Units who led the counterattack can choose from these newly cleaned guns. Throw away the old ones ... don't be shy ... there are as many guns as wood ... cleaning up the battlefield is tiring!" they joked.

Night falls. We fired one salvo.

Ah, Cook!

Bích arrived in the artillery bunker with a basket full of steaming sticky rice with beans.

"This is to congratulate you!" he said.

Mường Thanh has four zones. We've occupied two, and we're about to attack number three!

Infantry Divisions 312, 308, and 316 praised C804, and suggested Command Headquarters sends us merit papers.

April 2, 1954

A relatively quiet night at C804's command post. The People's Army, after three days of fighting, controls two of the four zones in Mường Thanh. The toughest French stronghold, Hill A1, resists.

Eldest Brother (Infantry Division 308) sent compliments to the artillery. The enemy parachuted five hundred 105mm shells into Eldest Brother's hands! Eldest Brother is storing them in the warehouse for the artillery.

Our batteries ran out of ammunition this afternoon. I saw artillerymen carrying ammunition back to Battery 4; Battery 2 seems to want to use the ammo immediately.

Review of the last three days of fighting

Four missions: contain enemy artillery, attack strongholds, finish the assaults, and repel enemy counterattacks ... Good, but not enough.

Hill A1[111] is more difficult than Hill D: the enemy is in underground bunkers.

The artillery must attack harder; officers must be flexible; economize ammunition, keep to normal daily routine and activities, and avoid complacency to create the right conditions for a General Attack.

The battery officers conducted a review:

Thể, a battery deputy leader, wasted ten shells! Write a review.

Xích didn't check the target range. He was distracted and careless; he miscalculated the angle by one hundred.

[The gunner] asked him: "It's 257, isn't it?"

[Xích] replied: "Yes."

He should have said: "No, it's 357 ..."

April 3, 1954
Another relatively quiet night at C804's command post across from Hill D.

Thế and Phục didn't get any sleep, thinking about what the General said about saving ammunition ... repairing dented shell casings to reuse them. Đăng pounded the casing with a hammer. He opened the breech to put it to the test.

"It works! It works!" he shouted.

"Remember to record the number of shells you've fixed in your

report!" Thắng, the company deputy leader, said with a smile.

Manager Thơm read out the financial statement, and hung it on the battery wall so that other brothers could see it.

Tạo wrote poems, sitting by a shell, while waiting for orders. Flares lit up the sky, their reflection on the shiny steel barrel sparkled inside the bunker. Artilleryman Number 8 looked through the sight device at the French green marker lights as minute as fireflies.

April 5, 1954
At the C804 command post across from Hill D. Accounts of the attack and counterattack against Hill D and of the attack against Hill C1.[112]

Report from the observation post at Noong Bua
[Preparing for the attack against Hill D,] Đức, Minh, Vạn, Cẩn were sent to dig trenches and artillery bunkers … Engineers followed. They helped carry wood back through one mile of trenches. They finished building the bunkers in four nights. The ground was hard, had to dig to set up the tripod. Afraid of not finishing on time, they went on digging through the night. They took advantage of the foggy morning to cut down trees to observe with the naked eye.

Dry air from the west wind from Laos. Gunners had to go a mile downhill to fetch rice … two miles to fill three waterbottles for two days!

[During the attack,] infantry soldiers stood in the trenches, in the rain. They were soaked … not enough tarpaulin.

When enemy artillery fired far away, the infantry kept advancing. There were loud cheers when Hill D was resolved.

… The enemy shot from four directions … our observation team was on watch when a paratrooper fell behind their post. A couple of comrades ran out with grenades.

The observation post is only a mile and a half from Mường Thanh. We're about two hundred yards from the enemy; we can see the enemy

Opposite: Entrance to a tunnel or shelter, 1954, graphite sketch on paper, 20 x 24cm. Collection of the artist.

131

clearly and vice versa ... Brothers on duty at the observation post crave books and newspapers.

Heard Phiên's story
[French counterattack against Hill D]
"The French soldiers didn't dare go out, they crapped in cans and threw them over the trench walls. When our artillerymen fired, the shit splashed everywhere, near corpses ...

"The enemy occupied one side of Hill D. We occupied the other side. In between were parachutes and an ammunition warehouse.

"The enemy didn't dare move up the hill where there were mines.

"Many comrades were killed: Tâm, the company deputy leader, and Huệ, the company deputy leader. Công lost a leg.

"We seized all the enemy 105mm ammunition in one night.

"Enemy infantry companies had tank[113] support as they went up the hill. Our artillery shot at the tanks from the front and the back. Our Soviet 82mm mortars set fire to a tank ... Another tank went back to Mường Thanh ... the enemy quickly withdrew ...

"A few puppet soldiers ... some had dark skin ... ran toward us and shouted they wanted to surrender ... The French fired ... wounded them.

"Last night, we occupied Hill 105 [north of the airstrip] and destroyed nine tanks. The enemy counterattacked with artillery shelling all day and all night. Their planes roared like barking dogs!"

Comrade Đức told me about the attack against the French stronghold, Hill C:

"Artillery from both sides fired from morning until noon (they had a company, we had a platoon). The enemy didn't dare leave [their shelters]. Then they all ran, got into vehicles, and disappeared. Planes dropped parachutes one-third of the distance between us and them. Some fell in between ... the enemy were afraid to pick them up. We fired at Mường Thanh ... everywhere was on fire. The enemy forced our compatriots to fill in the trenches we had just dug.

"[In the end], the enemy withdrew [from Hill C]."

At the command post, the ensemble entertained us with songs: "Farmers, rise up" ... "Green age" ... and a famous Chinese song ... The books we have to read include: *That's How Steel is Forged* by the Soviet writer Nikholai Ovstrosepki, *Thượng cam lĩnh*, a Chinese book about the North Korean Resistance Campaign, and *Most Beloved Ones* ... by Ngụy Nguyen.

Tâm summarizes the results of the second phase of the campaign. The People's Army has captured D1, D2, D3, C1, E1[114] and interdicted the enemy airfield, forcing enemy aircraft to make airdrops. Anti-aircraft guns have shot down fifty enemy aircraft. But the hardest battles have yet to come.

After the second phase of the battle
Assaulted more than five thousand enemy soldiers, one-third of the French Army! Over two thousand were killed.

The others are wounded, lying in underground shelters ... bandages are changed [only] every five days ...

We have completed the attack-and-siege phase.

We have effectively limited the activities of enemy aircraft.

We have tightened the siege around Điện Biên Phủ.

We've occupied many strong points and created good conditions for the General Assault.

On the enemy side:

Six guys share a loaf of bread and a can of food.

Three Legionnaires share a pack of biscuits and a loaf of bread a day.

Moroccan soldiers each get a bowl of rice with salted fish. No wine.

Puppet soldiers eat cooked rice and rice porridge.

No wood. They demolish the roof of their shelters for wood.

There's a shortage of officers.

Two gasoline depots and arsenals caught fire, and four cannons were damaged ...

Review of our experience:

Subjective and pessimistic attitude, lack of careful preparation.

Encourage a spirit of "endurance and continuous fighting."

Facsimile of diary pages dated April 7,
1954, featuring a sketch of anti-aircraft
defense artillerymen, 22 x 28cm.
Collection of the Điện Biên Phủ Museum.

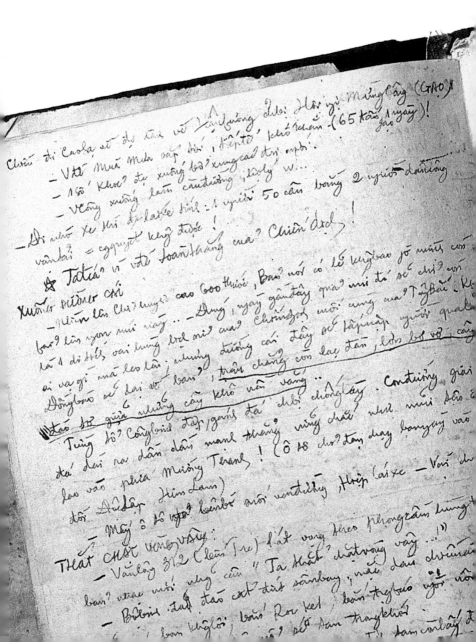

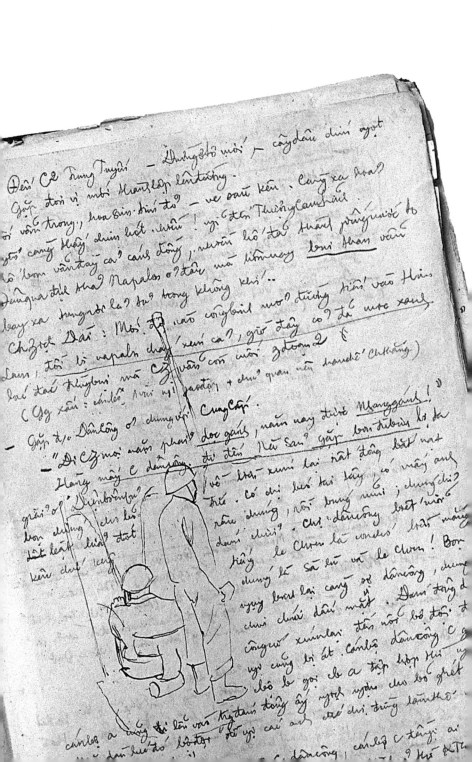

April 12, 1954

Tâm walks through the trenches from Hill D to the C828 anti-aircraft command post, on a mountain slope near Độc Lập.

Anti-aircraft gunners from C828 shot down a B24. The fiftieth plane shot down at Điện Biên! Just the other day, the General encouraged the artillery to compete to shoot down the fiftieth plane ... today C828 got it ... they were awarded a Second Class Military Merit Medal. Units send their congratulations.

The plane was burnt, black, but intact from wingtips to tail. We seized six heavy machine guns. Helmets, uniforms, guns of the dead ... a wallet with photographs of their wives and mothers in France ... Christian cards ... Indochina coins ...

During the night, enemy planes dropped dozens of parachutes with weapons near our battlefield ... white marks on our mountains and forests stained red from bomb craters.

Our trenches spread out like spider webs—from the high mountains down to the low fields of the Điện Biên Valley.

April 13, 1954

Tâm goes down to Tấu Village.[115] *The Thái village close to the front line had been destroyed by enemy bombings.*

Tấu Village

Slanted houses, about to collapse. Tattered thatch. Broken beams, columns, bare and charred. Rice mortars dried by sunlight. Mango and jackfruit trees twisted, cracked ... broken, withered ... amputated and marked by bullets ...

Opposite: Soldier aiming a bayonet,
Điện Biên Phủ, 1954, graphite sketch
on paper, 20 x 28cm. Private collection.

Back at the C828 anti-aircraft command post, Lộc, Battery 1 officer, encouraged everyone to write letters home:

"Everyone has their own emotions and feelings … we should write letters to our families to tell them about our success [shooting down the fiftieth plane] …"

A soldier showed me his letter:

"Letter from Hiền on the battlefield to my beloved Cầm:

Dear Cầm,

Since the day I left home, I haven't had a chance to write.

Now I'm writing to you and our son Thiện to let you know how I am.

I'm very happy to know both of you are healthy.

As for me, I'm fine, fighting at Điện Biên Phủ.

Life is very happy, my darling. I've learned to operate AA guns, and am trying to shoot down enemy planes.

Perhaps you've heard about my unit's success?

Look after Thiện for me … remember.

I have a lot to tell you when we meet again.

Take care, my darling.

I'm writing while fighting, so I can't write much more.

Send my best to Mom and to the neighbors …"

We were out of paper, asked for more from the others.

The battery leader wrote his letter half in verse, half in prose. He read aloud as he wrote … Như wrote his letter crouched under the gun platform, his bottom sticking out. Dua wrote on his thigh, on the platform seat.

Others wrote by the wheels of the cannon.

Comrade X wasn't writing.

"Don't ask ... my family is in Hải Dương,[116] temporarily occupied by the enemy. I wrote once but I didn't receive a letter back ..." he explained.

"You're not doing the right thing ... You need to write," we told him.

"It's fun to help each other write. Let me write it for you ... to my beloved wife ..." Comrade Giảng joked.

Comrade Tụ came from Bắc Giang Province in the Resistance Zone. He knew about the Party's Mass Mobilization efforts to introduce the Land Reform Program. But he didn't know about its success. Still, he ended his letter with a poem holding the occupation responsible for our suffering:

"To Father and Stepmother ...

Today thanks to the Party and Uncle, I've made a lot of progress.

I expressed my suffering to accuse landlords (tố khổ). I realize how miserable my situation was before. Now that I have food and clothes, please don't worry about me, and concentrate on running the farm:

I'm grown up now and mature ...

The enemy is the cause of our family's suffering ...

I hope to kill the enemy on the battlefield ...

We attack in spite of bombs and bullets, of wind and dew ... facing hardship and death. Family, don't worry about me, and focus on growing food ..."

April 14, 1954

At the C828 anti-aircraft command post near Độc Lập Hill.

I read many letters written by our dear soldiers in the trenches. They give me the letters to read before they lick the envelope. Not because I'm clever like the political commissar of the Russian Red Army who had "a key to open souls ..." I watched the film a few days before the campaign ... Here, facing the enemy head on, about to be killed at any moment by a shell fired from an enemy bunker or random shell fragments, we don't think about life and death anymore. Only us and them.

Code 7A has great meaning here: the love for comrades, and friendship on this side of the trenches, the love for Thái, Mèo, and Việt Bắc ethnic groups, and the love of our homeland, for all our people behind the lines waiting for victory. The whole democratic world is supporting us, hoping we will destroy colonialism! In every fortification, trench, or bunker, I meet ME-US (*TA*)! We've never personally met before, but we're ready to pour our hearts out to each other.

A letter from the rear to the front:

"Reading news about Điện Biên Phủ, everyone wants to know whether you've shot down another plane?"

This question was never asked before. Our people were so used to being attacked and suppressed from above … for so long!

And another letter from an artilleryman to his parents:

"Father and Mother,

I'm honored to learn how to fire anti-aircraft guns and to have joined the Điện Biên Phủ Campaign. This is the greatest honor of my life. I'm fighting. Enemy planes drop many bombs, but we remain calm and shoot accurately to protect our infantry … The more enemy planes we shoot down, the fewer planes will be bombing the rear."

The letter is both emotional and practical, and matches our people's expectations and our own.

With the anti-aircraft artillery

Hills and mountains were bare and red, or covered in white, charred earth. Fields are ploughed up around bomb craters. Soil is dried yellow. Our anti-aircraft artillery has dug their fortifications in the bomb craters. They've camouflaged them with straw.

Officers and fighters are young, with rosy, sunburnt cheeks. Their iron helmets are smeared with soil. Most are poor farmers who volunteered to join the Army. Their job is to sit on the gun tray, read the newspaper, and wait for enemy aircraft.

Many come from Hải Dương Province in occupied territory. When they first saw the big guns and began training, they were scared, worried how they would "manage" these things … During training, they thought it was easier to shoot planes flying straight than dive-bombing … But after a few fights, they changed their minds.

"Let the plane come down, and when it's facing us, easy to shoot and terrify it. It's a battle of wills!" a gunner told me.

Sitting on the revolving battery platform, they cheer when a plane is hit ... they lower the gun barrels during firing pauses to readjust the firing ranges.

The artillery has "no front line and no support at the back."

The villages around the bomb craters are deserted. The only sign they ever existed are jackfruit, orange, and peach trees with green fruit, and amaranth (*rau dền*, used to make soup) covering the ground. A lone mortar, overturned ... Scattered pieces of an indigo shirt and a quilted blanket next to an American napalm bomb.

"Enemy planes coming! Direction 12 ... speed 190, fire at the one in the middle!"

"... lock the target!"

The whistle blew! Fire!

I read a letter to a soldier sent from the rear:

"Gratitude! During the 1952 Fall–Winter campaign, the soldiers of the People's Army liberated over ten thousand square miles in the Northwest and captured six thousand enemy soldiers. In 1953, our Army killed three thousand bandits in Lai Châu, Thuận Châu ... Thanks to our Army, thousands of people were liberated. Other minority groups Thái, Mán, Xá, Mèo ... were rescued ... People contributed ten thousand tons of rice, meat, and vegetables to the campaign."

April 15, 1954
At the C827 anti-aircraft artillery command post near Độc Lập Hill. Tâm records a deadly attack by enemy artillery and fighter bombers.

Digging trenches
We intercepted information between French pilots and their Command Center in Mường Thanh:

"Việt Minh anti-aircraft artillery is near Độc Lập. Request counterattacks from our artillery."

We dug trenches aggressively and urgently to protect the guns.

The enemy fired seven artillery rounds.

Diên, the battery commander, was injured.

He remained calm and kept encouraging the unit.

After checking the range finder, the company ordered everyone to get ready ... Brothers stood on the gun platforms and promised to record their exploits for the Party, Uncle Hồ.

Barking enemy planes dive-bombed onto our battlefield: eight Hen Cats, two B24s, eight B26s. Bombs all around us!

We stayed calm and fired.

Lương, from the typographic squadron, reported ...

Hiền and Chừng, two very young soldiers, loaded ammunition.

Lộc shouted words of encouragement over the explosions.

"Our families, our dead comrades need revenge! Kill 'em all!" he cried.

Enemy artillery fired close by.

"Nhuận has been killed!"

Above, the very blue sky was sultry, filled with the burning smell of guns, bombs ... Enemy planes took advantage of the blazing sunlight ... and came at us from the direction of the sun.

Seeing danger ... comrades felt anxious.

April 16, 1954
At the C827 anti-aircraft artillery command post near Độc Lập Hill.

Next day's battle: one gun out of action, two guns blocked.

Urgent repairs were made.

Our gunners got back on the gun platform and continued firing.

Average range-firing guns were blocked ...

They calmly encouraged each other.

"We're not afraid!" they shouted.

Battery 1 was the only battery left to counterattack ...

From noon to 5 p.m.

The political commissar told the brothers to stand firm.

After Nhuận was killed, the battery commander was killed.

Trấn immediately took command of Battery 1. He received a Third Class Glorious Soldier Medal.

A comrade suggested retreating.

"No retreat. Stay with the guns," Lộc said.

Sounds of cheering. An enemy plane was hit, wounded, it's a Hellcat. It fled, a trail of smoke at its tail.

Over three hundred bombs were dropped on our battlefield!

Battery 1 received a Second Class Glorious Exploit Medal. Lộc got a Third Class Glorious Soldier Medal.

"From our experience:

"Never leave the gun platform! And shoot accurately!"

Enemy planes took advantage of the sunlight. They dive-bombed and attacked our battlefield.

Bombs, shells, fire, and smoke, soil, and dust covered the fields.

Niển, Chừng loaded shells.

Soil covered the gun sight … they couldn't even see the gun barrel.

More gunners were injured by bombs. The political commissar rushed to dig them out.

Battery 1 was back in action.

Trấn, the Third Medal winner, continued commanding Battery 1.

It was a ferocious battle … but most of our soldiers coming from peasant backgrounds … they have learned to "express their grievances" … this is the place to seek revenge, revenge for their class, their people, and their family. They are showing their determination to win!

There's Hoàng Đình Lộc, Number 6 in Battery 1, from a poor farmer family in Thanh Trì, near Hanoi; Hoàng Văn Phác, who held up a bridge with his shoulders for trucks to pass over on Route 13 in 1953; and Ma Văn Rạch, who carried artillery guns barefoot.

And here in Điện Biên Phủ, the brave fighter Tô Vĩnh Diện who sacrificed himself, acting as a human wedge to prevent the gun from falling downhill. The gun got here safely.

C727 scored a hit and shot down a plane.

The French pilot dropped his bombs and flew away, but the plane was hit by our bullets and exploded in mid-air.

In the afternoon, the anti-aircraft artillerymen received instruction to go to the rear to celebrate their success.

Problems

The rainy season is coming! There are supply shortages.

Rice! We need sixty-five tons a day!

Healthy and strong soldiers are called to supplement new units.

Singers from the performing groups join to help build bridges, roads, and serve as nurses … Drivers calculate: pick up one person weighing one hundred and ten pounds or two [skinny] civic workers for the sake of a victorious campaign!

Going to the main road

Tâm is ordered to return to the artillery division headquarters at the back of the battlefield where he stays for a few days.

Looking up at the Command Headquarters two thousand feet up.

"Maybe we'll never have to go up this mountain again," Lý Thái Bảo reflected. [Lý Thái Bảo was a well-known film director who served as a liaison officer and political commissar with the anti-aircraft artillery regiment during the Điện Biên Phủ Campaign.]

Correct. One day soon, this mountain will be a historic relic from the last campaign of the Northwest … no reason to climb it.

One day this main road will be open, crowded with people and vehicles. People will return to their villages. Buffaloes will no longer stray from their herds. Pigs will no longer stand in a dry and desolate landscape of desiccated peach trees.

Engineer teams were breaking up rocks. They carried them in baskets to pack the roads to prevent flooding. Reinforced roads are like a boat's bow that can ride the waves straight to Mường Thanh.

Vehicles transported ammunition to Độc Lập, Him Lam in daylight. Enemy planes are being sucked into Mường Thanh.

Trucks stopped by the river near the roadside for a rest.

Women civic workers were washing their hair and clothes in the river. They joked, happy and noisy.

I listened to the sound of the stream again, rushing, flowing. The water is so clear and blue.

And my own happiness: I've received permission to go back to the front line!

❧

Tighten the siege

The F312 performing troops [Infantry Division 312, code name Bến Tre] played a new song on the accordion: "We're tightening the siege."

Our infantry dug trenches across the airfield. Enemy planes keep bombing, shooting rockets, shelling, and laying mines with time-delay fuses. Red dots shriek through the air and explode into black smoke.

The enemy airdropped supplies. We collected more than half of the parachuted supplies. Most are scattered in the middle of the airfield, white dots on the airstrip.

We resolved Hill 105. The enemy counterattacked. But we intercepted their reinforcements!

I ran into "Doctor Thu" at Long Châu [the code name for Artillery Division 351]. He looked so strange but we were happy to see each other. Thu is devoted to the campaign, but he doesn't love his job. Maybe because he doesn't get to go to the front line much? Yes, the most attractive place in battle is the front line, face to face with the enemy.

To the middle wing
Ripe and very sweet blackberries … I met a new unit, they were already marching … Rose myrtle with purple-red *sim* flowers.[117] Cicadas are singing. The further away from the front line, the more songbirds there are … There are bomb craters everywhere in the fields. Craters are filled with water in ponds of different sizes.

Last night, enemy planes must have dropped napalm. Wood ash lingered in the air.

I remember the days when sappers opened the way to Him Lam and the hills were burnt by napalm. But the grass there is green again.

Today the campaign is at the end of the second phase. I also knew that a few officers fluctuated between being negative and positive, so there were limits to our success.[118]

April 18, 1954
At the headquarters of the artillery division. Tâm talks to civic workers supplying the front.

I met some civic workers. They said that last year they "went to the front line" on narrow paths up steep slopes and shortcuts. But this year they can "mooch off" the roads our vehicles use to transport the artillery. On their way to Điện Biên, they met prisoners of war captured in Điện Biên and taken to the rear … Men and women surrounded the prisoners. They bullied them to blow off some steam … a woman pinched a Westerner's ear. Someone pulled his beard. One flicked his nose … Another called them *salaud* (*xa lu*) and *le chien* (*lo-xieng*). The prisoners complained but didn't dare talk back.

Puppet soldiers were even more afraid of these civic workers.

In the end, our soldiers had to intervene.

"Stop! Sisters, it's a violation of our policy!" an officer said.

Opposite: Soldier with the pickaxe used for digging tunnels, Điện Biên Phủ, 1954, sketch, ink on notebook paper, 6 x 8cm. Collection of the Ho Chi Minh City Fine Arts Museum.

He finally suggested that those who acted wrongly should do their self-criticism. They all raised their hands.

"OK, all of us will do our self-criticism!" they shouted.

"I didn't want to break Party rules, but they all deserve to be tied up and shot," one of them added.

What the civic workers did was wrong. But their actions come from the people's desire for revenge!

April 20, 1954

At the headquarters. Accounts from civic workers from Mường Pú, a village near the front that had been burned to the ground in December 1953.

Xá civic workers from Mường Pú reported:

"We refused to follow the French down the mountain. There we would starve to death! The enemy burned our fields. We ploughed on far away land and found manioc in the jungle, but we didn't have enough to eat."

Lò Thị Vy, a young girl, was too young but insisted she wanted to join the civic workers. Very innocent. On the Nà Pứu Pass, dewdrops made the path slippery. She forgot she was tired. She cut bamboo, and stretched it into a lyre, playing and singing along the way.

Civic workers from Vĩnh Phúc went to Na Mường [a hundred miles from Vĩnh Phúc] to show the Thái how to make rice-pounding mills. Pestles are slow and outdated. Using rice-pounding mills shows unity [between the ethnic people and the People's Army]. Villagers and civic workers joined to dance and sing: "Unite" [a poem by Uncle Hồ].

Lyrics:

Up and down, brothers and sisters

Share rice with the Vietnamese

One heart: South–North–West–East

Clasp hands under one flag of struggle

Rub clean the stinking seeds

In plains and mountains, of the same green once again …

A woman asked our soldiers to be careful and avoid hitting others, but she made a slip of the tongue and said "beat" instead of "avoid."

The soldiers teased her:

"If you beat us, we'll ask for compensation."

"What compensation?"

"We'll beat you back ..."

April 21, 1954

At the headquarters of the artillery division.

Lân gave us a report on the general situation.

"Mr Molotov[119] delivered a speech in Geneva on two important issues: the five big powers versus Vietnam, and North Korea.

"Enemy in Điện Biên:

"More than two-thirds of enemy-parachuted supplies fell to our side, ammunition for 60mm mortars, and boxes, cans of food ... Soil is crumbled and loose from bomb explosions.

"We destroyed two companies and an enemy tank when we attacked 206. The central Mường Thanh battlefield has shrunk to one-third of a square mile!

"Our network of trenches helped prevent injuries when we attacked, so our soldiers feel very confident. Trenches crisscross Hill D all the way to Mường Thanh.

"Our intelligence units closely followed enemy action, all missions accomplished! The enemy carries wood for more than three miles to build fortifications. They are more and more exposed, with nowhere to find wood.

"Our anti-aircraft artillery controls the enemy airfield; our trenches are getting closer to Hồng Cúm [the largest enemy fortress after Mường Thanh, with a second airstrip, five miles to the south of Mường Thanh].

"We are gradually surrounding the whole of Điện Biên Phủ!"

The People's Army has been preparing for the third coordinated barrage against the toughest French strongholds, the French headquarters, and the airfield. The siege has tightened. The People's Army network of trenches has joined up with enemy trenches. Tâm was aware that some high-ranking

147

officers doubted victory was possible: soldiers have been fighting for a month; they have suffered huge casualties, and are physically and mentally exhausted.
The third coordinated barrage is planned for the evening of May 1.

April 30, 1954
On the eve of the third attack, Tâm returns to the front, to the command post of the C755 mountain artillery on Hill E. C755 occupied Hill E on March 30 and have been defending it against French counterattacks for a month.

7 a.m., playing poker (*Tú-lơ-khơ*).

The first shot by one of our units hit an enemy post. Black smoke covered the mound, creating a focal point for our guns to target.

The officers seemed very nervous. They had clear assignments. On a larger scale, minute by minute …

Mừng, Number 2, hasn't mastered firing techniques because he's just moved from a transportation unit, but he shows self-control and pays attention.

Mr Hoàng Cao came by.

"Wishing all comrades great achievements to celebrate May 1! Comrades, do you remember that tomorrow is May 1?" he asked.

Brothers were reassembling a gun, an officer helped them carry the Soviet 82mm mortars up to the observation post.

Army ordnance was moved to the foot of Him Lam, across a field full of thorns, worm-like leeches … through mud, marshes.

The enemy fired sporadic shots from half a mile away. Point-blank shots, red like burning, hot coals, tore across the dark sky. The fog was thick and rain clouds flashed across the sky.

Enemy planes dropped parachutes more often in the evening.

Our anti-aircraft guns fired continuously.

Tonight, we didn't have time to dig shelters, so I'm sleeping outside in the fog—"on earthen pillows," listening to the sound of guns …

The enemy knew we had set up a new battlefield and attacked us immediately. Our fortifications collapsed. There was only a hole left. The whole battery climbed out, laughing, cursing the enemy. We began building shelters again, determined to stay in place.

In the early morning, I walked down the hill. A small stream meanders to the right behind the hill toward the Nậm Rốm River and the Mường Thanh Bridge. Leafy tree branches quivered over the water's surface … a rare place of beauty the enemy artillery can't reach.

It's also the place where after a night of digging trenches, fighting … returning filthy, covered in mud … the infantrymen jump into the stream to bathe. They sit down to eat rice and loaves of bread captured from the enemy, and divide up parachute fabric. They sleep. Then they return to their units, regroup, and set off at night to fight in the Central Zone.

The C755 mountain artillery have been defending Hill E for a whole month, it's a very important high point. They are face to face with the enemy's heavy artillery in Mường Thanh and the airfield.

After the mountain artillery captured and occupied Hill E, they strengthened the fortifications so enemy 155mm artillery shells[120] couldn't penetrate them.

Their firing range is wide. They see the enemy clearly, and fire straight shots. Sometimes they fire first, sometimes the enemy does. When they see enemy tanks coming, they fire first.

Despite the constant daily stress of being so close to the enemy, the C755 artillerymen have taken the time to decorate their bunkers, even more than units who are further away from the enemy. The tunnels and trench walls are all white, covered with the fabric of enemy parachutes and flares (flare parachutes).

May 4, 1954
At the command post of the mountain artillery C755 on Hill E.

Encouragement from the General
Consolidate and expand victory.
Efforts to fight and reorganize forces.
Create conditions to destroy all the enemy at Điện Biên Phủ.
Two-fifths of the enemy killed, five tanks, fifty aircraft!
Guns of all sizes were fired at the enemy.
We cut communication between Mường Thanh and Hồng Cúm.
Enemy morale is low.

There are supply shortages.

Thousands of wounded soldiers are trapped. Navarre, De Castries[121] strongly suggested ... The enemy is very afraid of our artillery, even of our rifles and snipers.

Reasons for our success so far

The Central Military Commission was correct:

Our army was brave.

Fought firmly, advanced firmly.

Built an attack-and-siege battlefield.

Attacked strong enemy bases.

However, we don't have good enough conditions for the General Attack for the following reasons:

Some officers and units haven't fulfilled their missions.

There are over seven thousand enemy soldiers, and one stronghold in the east, Hill A. The enemy has supplies, reinforcements, and a powerful artillery.

New missions

Continue to build attack-and-siege battlefields.

Improve the terrain to tighten the siege, destroy enemy supplies and reinforcements. Increase the threat to completely cut off communication between Mường Thanh and Hồng Cúm.

We must keep our battlefield positions solid for a relatively long time.

Fight bravely to destroy the enemy:

1. Attack the enemy, counterattack tanks and artillery.

2. Control Điện Biên Phủ airspace day and night, seize, limit, and wipe out enemy supplies.

3. Attack and destroy the airfield, creating conditions to occupy and control the airfield.

4. Organize small units of snipers and marksmen, mobile gunners to attack. Together, small units will produce a larger one.

5. Destroy several enemy positions, counterattack continuously, destroy and block reinforcements. Request: destroy.

Reorganize and maintain soldiers' physical and mental strength.

Unite new and veteran soldiers with initiatives to improve food and living conditions. Prevent disease, save ammunition, maintain discipline on the battlefield.

Strike and learn from experience. Carry out the slogan: "Move one step further after each battle!"

Completing all four missions will result in the loss of three enemy strengths, creating the right conditions for the General Attack.

Raise your determination to continue fighting for the final victory of the campaign!

Understand its great and important meaning.

Determined to fight against subjectivity and complacency.

Don't panic or waver in difficulties, don't be afraid of losing energy and being exhausted, always fight bravely and persistently.

The entire Army, the people, the Communist Party, Uncle Hồ, the Central Military Commission, and the world are waiting for our victory at Điện Biên Phủ!

May 5, 1954
At the command post of the mountain artillery C753 on Hill E1. Tâm learns from the artillerymen about their dramatic attack against Hill D on March 30 and Hill C on May 1.

Going to the mountain artillery
The 75mm guns are less than half a mile from the enemy. The artillery have suffered more casualties when building fortifications than when fighting.

Comrades Liên, Đắc, Chúc ...

Đính, company deputy leader.

Huyến, the political commissar, said he's new to C753. He's getting to know a few more soldiers every day (good, bad, average):

"We don't understand each other yet, but in times of difficulty and danger we will. The infantry, artillery, and anti-aircraft gunners live in harmony and understanding. Infantrymen carry wood to help the artillerymen build fortifications."

A platoon leader of the mountain artillery [gives Tâm an account of their attack against Hill D on March 30 and Hill C on May 1]:

"Yên, the battery leader, observed the structure of Hill D. We based our attack points on the different types of enemy shelters identified."

He continued:

"9 p.m. The enemy fired three 105mm. Thời and the cannon were buried. My brothers and I managed to pull them out. We had to abandon the shelter.

"Hoàng went deaf from the blast.

"We built another shelter.

"The enemy shelled again.

"Again we abandoned the shelter ... 4 a.m. we built another shelter:

—No matter how many times they fire, we'll destroy them!

"Đắc's legs were blown up in the minefield on Hill D ... very painful, but he was happy the brothers completed the mission.

—The Party assigned the mission, but I haven't finished yet. Help me finish, please! said Brother Đắc, a new Party member.

"Results: three enemy gun emplacements were hit, three 120mm guns and one machine-gun nest destroyed!

"An artilleryman was subjective and overconfident: he went outside the shelter for food and was killed by an enemy bomb on April 24.

"[On May 1, we were ordered to attack Hill C:]

"7:22 a.m. May 1, 1954.

"Fire, control the enemy so the infantry can attack.

"Non-stop firing for three or four days. Sometimes three, sometimes four, up to twenty-six shells.

"In four hours, both guns shot fifty-six times.

"The next day, the enemy guessed the time and counterattacked. One shell emitted poisonous gas. The gas lingered for six hours. The wing of the gun bunker collapsed ... No casualties.

"We temporarily retreated to avoid the gas.

"But in the evening we went back to reinforce the bunker after the infantry was ordered to launch an attack early the next morning.

"The political commissar, Huyến, went up first. No smell of gas. The wind direction had changed and was blowing toward the enemy. He decided there was no danger. He ordered everyone to wear gauze masks and to get the fortifications ready.

"We all helped reinforce the artillery shelters.

"The infantry ordered the artillery to fire for fifteen minutes and destroy three enemy bunkers ... the artillery destroyed the bunkers in just eight shots.

"The enemy counterattacked and cut off communication lines.

"Đệ and Đôn rushed out, found the lines, and reconnected them.

"7:20 a.m. Order from the captain to go to the observation post.

"The political commissar held the receiver and listened:

—The General orders us to demolish the fort on Hill C!

"Nervous. We checked the guns. They were blocked ... Thăng jumped out to unblock them.

"7:22 a.m. Order to fire. We fired four times.

"As soon as the firing stopped, our infantry rushed up to the flagpole ... the two attack forces (artillery and infantry) met.

"Some enemy soldiers were captured, others killed.

Quy hadn't believed in infantry regiment 176.[122]

—I didn't expect the unit to be so strong, he said.

Remarks by Huyền the political commissar:

"Experience shows that soldiers who stand upright, observe carefully, and speak out ... are the brave ones.

"Experience from the battle in Tu Vũ[123]: artillerymen advanced in four lines under fire from enemy artillery. During times of intense tension, saying a word, a sentence ... that's good ... Even a sentence can encourage the others, and show calm, courage ... at that time silence is a psychological struggle between life and death:

—I'm about to get hurt ... am I hurt?

"But the artillerymen carrying heavy loads were out of breath and couldn't talk. And ethnic brothers don't talk much.

"Whereas the three-men infantry units[124] shouted at each other:

—Is he up yet? Are you up yet?

—Tell him to be strong and move forward!!!

"They shouted to hear over the loud explosions. Shouting may be rude at other times, but in combat helps drown out the fear in your mind."

Soldiers by the stream behind Hill E, 1954, watercolor on paper, 39 x 35cm. Collection of the artist.

May 6, 1954

At the command post of the mountain artillery on Hill E1, "less than half a mile from the enemy." Tâm meets Phùng Văn Khầu, a legendary mountain artilleryman of the campaign.[125] *Phùng Văn Khầu joined the Việt Minh at the young age of ten in 1940 and the Army in 1949. He had distinguished himself in every campaign of the war before he was selected to be part of the artillery division during the Điện Biên Phủ Campaign.*

An infantryman stopped by the mountain artillery command post. He told us about the May 1 attack:

"The artillery was shooting with guns of different calibers: recoiless rifles, artillery, and rockets … you hit the enemy loopholes and black smoke filled their bunkers. The enemy fell. They were hit again with our Soviet 82mm mortars. They ran shouting:

—Damn it! Damn it!

"That night we cleared four enemy posts."

… The artillerymen were having food. They invited the infantryman to join them. At first he behaved as a "guest," but when he saw there was enough rice, he sat down, and ate like a family member.

[Later, I met up with] Phùng Văn Khầu. He is an outstanding "character" of the mountain artillery unit. At twenty-five years old, the squadron officer has participated in all our campaigns from the Border Campaign to the Điện Biên Phủ Campaign, and has two Third Class Soldier Medals.

The mountain artillery occupies Hill E1

Khầu led his men uphill under intense enemy artillery fire. He couldn't see anything through the dark smoke. He fumbled around, looking for the others … making sure they were alive.

Lying close to the ground, Khầu and his men built fortifications. It took them three nights to complete the bunkers.[126]

They dug with both hands, shovelling, and clearing the soil by hand even though their hands were swollen.

Being very near the enemy, they dug secretly at night.

Sometimes Khầu stood up while the enemy was firing.

When the explosions stopped, they continued digging quietly so the enemy couldn't hear them.

Pulling the cannons into the fortifications

It was rainy and wet, very tiring. They were seven including Khầu. They hauled the guns up from the foot of the hill [in parts, a 75mm pack Howitzer gun weighed a thousand pounds]—it's OK to lose a few pounds of rice, but can't lose five tons of steel, not even a screw!

It was tough on the slopes. They were only two men for each cannon instead of four. Five times …

Gunners and mortars were covered in mud. Going up the hill in daytime, the enemy could easily spot them. They had to pass the gun parts lying down. Barrels, axles, wheels, and boxes with spare parts … over their bodies … and down into the mouth of the underground bunker! In they go!

The men then went back down a thousand feet to fetch water to clean the guns. Reassemble, unblock the barrels … Ready. Khầu learned from a companion unit: unblock the gun barrel one more time to be sure.

Report:

"Occupation completed, secret kept."

The infantry regiment sent praise.

Enter combat

Required to cut down their numbers (Numbers 5, 6, 2, 1, 3 are left). Khầu doubled as leader and Number 4, who rotates the elevating hand-wheel, clears the barrel, disperses smoke, checks the gun sight.

First result: twenty-eight shots, only two shots were low. And all hit their targets. The infantry charged. Success!

Order to withdraw: the enemy fired non-stop. So close to the enemy, the lid of a shelter was hit, and the beams were shattered.

Khầu told the men to disperse while he stayed with the gun to protect the range finder. He wrapped the gun parts in blankets and tarpaulin on his own … then joined the others.

Khầu returned to the bunker the next day to see if there was anything left. He found pickaxes, two shovels, and brought back five cartridges.

I asked Khầu what he thinks of when he's alone.

Khẩu remembers what his father told him when he left home:
"Try your best to fulfill your mission, don't be troublesome."
Khẩu promised.

Enemy counterattack against Hill E1
The enemy counterattacked. Numbers 1 and 2 were injured.

The unit built five fortifications with covers. They took turns cutting down trees and carried the wood at night.

Khẩu was promoted to deputy platoon and served as Number 2 for the Japanese gun[127] because there was no replacement. The newly added Number 1 had to get used to the American gun.[128]

"Pull the trigger straight after each shot," Khẩu reminded him.

The mountain artillery unit fought seven consecutive battles, destroyed enemy gun emplacements, and three enemy 105mm guns. Recommended for a Third Class Soldier Medal. That was in the third battle.

Fourth battle
Khẩu and our artillery were a third of a mile from the enemy. Enemy 105mm barrels were clearly visible. The enemy fired 12mm machine guns. Our cannons rumbled. The enemy went silent and retreated.

The enemy then fired three shots. Their loophole collapsed. Khẩu and Pao immediately went out to fix it. Brothers also offered, not afraid of enemy bullets. They continued firing and destroyed five enemy gun emplacements at the 203 position.

Fifth battle
Pao is Number 2. The mountain artillery unit fired five shots and destroyed two enemy gun emplacements. The enemy machine-gunned and injured the new Number 1 from C752.

Sixth battle
The gunners reinforced their fortification all night.

In the morning, they rested and had some food.

At noon, they were ordered to reassemble the guns.

1 p.m., order to go into battle.

"Let's stay as calm as yesterday!" Nghiếm said.

Only three of them were left to fight this battle.

Pao opened the breech.

Khầu took aim.

Nghiếm wasn't familiar with this gun.

He didn't pull the trigger straight …

"Hold the end of the rope straight. Count the seconds, when I say 'Pull!' you pull …" Khầu instructed him.

Nghiếm hit the left edge of the enemy fortification.

"Shoot again, remember pull straight!"

They fired six shots and hit three enemy fortifications. The company had assigned them a quota of five.

But an enemy smoke shell hit their loophole.

The blast hit all three of them: Khầu, Pao, and Nghiếm. They couldn't breathe. They passed out. When Khầu came to, he couldn't see anything. He stretched out to try to find the range finder. Then he crawled out of the bunker and called the others. No one answered. He crawled back in, called for a while … Pao and Nghiếm finally came out of the underground shelter. Pao tried to walk to the trench wall. He passed out again. His eyes were closed. He wasn't breathing.

Khầu and Nghiếm thought Pao was dead. They cried. They shook him and called him. Finally, Pao came to. They carried him to the vaulted entrance of the shelter so he could rest.

Then another shell hit their fortifications.

"Our gun is damaged!" Khầu told Pao.

Khầu continued to hold onto the range finder.

Khầu was sad and tired.

He chewed a rice ball to regain energy.

They didn't want to leave the bunker … until they received a third order from the company:

"Officers must dismantle the guns and temporarily withdraw down the hill."

At the command post, when Khầu and Pao realized the enormous casualties in team 2, they cried.

Seventh battle

Khầu encouraged Pao and Nghiếm to send "blood letters" to the company, promising to avenge their unit.

Violent enemy counterattacks continued.

The breech … Trung and Tưởng jumped out of the underground shelter to shovel soil away. Everyone stayed very calm.

The shelter collapsed again. They jumped out to shovel again, and prepare to fire.

Our gunners destroyed four enemy fortifications in this battle.

Eighth battle

They carried guns up the hill again, cleaned them, and put them into the old gun emplacements right across from the enemy. The terrain was bare. Enemy air raids against Hill E had destroyed the trenches.

Three carried guns across land heavily damaged by bombs and shells … pulled in front … pushed at the back."

Khẩu was ordered back to the company command post.

Comrade Tưởng was sent as Number 2.

Enemy tanks fired …

*Molotova trucks transported us back from
Điện Biên Phủ to the military base in
Tuyên Quang*, 1954, wash on paper,
16 x 24cm. Collection of the artist.

Tưởng was killed.

Another comrade replaced him.

At headquarters, Khầu was worried, afraid that the new Number 2 wasn't ready … he asked to go back into battle. He immediately destroyed enemy fortifications with only one shot. He was recalled again and sent to help another unit.

In one battle, he served as artillerymen Numbers 1, 2, 3, 4, and 5.

Khầu:

"Once I was very hungry. I was about to eat some rice, when an enemy shell hit. Soil rained down. The rice was full of dirt. I stayed hungry!"

Khầu laughed, he slapped his thighs, and clouds of dust flew up in the air.

On duty on top of that hill, day and night, he had no time to go down to the stream at the back of the hill.

Going Home

May 7, 1954
At the command post of the mountain artillery on Hill E.

Yesterday evening, when it was dark, I went through the trenches and fields from Hill D to Hill E where I stayed with the mountain artillery unit. I suddenly met soldiers setting up a strange-looking gun: long tubes joined together.

During the night, I had heard thunder bursts, as though giant flocks of birds swooped down on Mường Thanh ... the explosion was deafening.

Terrifying!

I found out it was an H12 Russian Katyusha,[129] the rocket launcher that petrified German fascists during World War II.

This morning, I met infantrymen who had attacked the enemy's rear last night. I asked what the weapon was, but nobody answered. They shook their heads, laughed, and pointed to their ears. Our soldiers were deaf. They had been so close to the explosion.

Last night we occupied Hill A1—the toughest stronghold, and most of the hills this side of the Nậm Rốm River.

This morning we continued to attack the Central Zone. I understood

Opposite: Flowers and damaged helmet, Điện Biên Phủ,
May 1953, watercolor on letter-writing paper, 23 x 18cm.
Collection of the artist.

this was the General Attack. Here, on Hill E, I meet everyone, clearly see the enemy dead ... the more our artillery attacks, the more we win and "bully" the enemy, destroy them, and silence them.

I have a clear overview of the battlefield! The Nậm Rốm River is filled with litter, white parachutes fall from the iron bridge ... some enemy soldiers went to get water and were sniped ... during the days at the command and observation posts, I also knew about the general situation.

I was attracted by the tense events, the explosion of bombs and bullets, all the fighting going on around Hill E and the Nậm Rốm River ... until late in the afternoon, when the gunfire died down, it seemed to calm down, or was it tense again, as if waiting for something ...

When from over a mound, an infantry soldier walked toward me with heavy steps. He was exhausted, collapsed, and only said a few words:

"Victory at last!"

The infantry had deployed troops to attack when they met the enemy surrendering in Mường Thanh! With De Castries!

Cheers rang out, echoed over fields, red barren hills ... These small infantrymen were victorious!

So happy! They rushed [into the Central Zone]! (Young soldiers who hadn't seen combat yet: "Resentful!")

Enemy soldiers came flooding out of Mường Thanh. Puppet soldiers in motley uniforms, Westerners in white, some in their underwear [*si líp,* from the French *slip*] ... iron helmets, plastic helmets, discarded in fields.

Just after 5 p.m., after a series of rockets and fires in Mường Thanh and Hồng Cúm, the enemy waved white flags made from parachute fabric![130] They crept out of their "crab" holes, hands up, holding white handkerchiefs to surrender ...

They crossed the river ... They came out of their shelters, stood up, shouting because they were happy to escape from their tombs.

One of our officers stood on a mound, waving to show them the way. They stood in line, obediently bowing their heads. No one resisted or retreated ... no way out!

A soldier raised the *Determined to fight, Determined to win* flag ... an officer spoke through a simple loudspeaker he had brought with him ... French and puppet soldiers raised their heads, listened.

De Castries had intended to drive out in a jeep to surrender. But faced with the guns of our soldiers right inside his headquarters, he raised his hands, was forced onto a truck, and taken to the Command Headquarters.[131] Officers–soldiers, blacks–whites, and yellow (skin color) were divided into four lines.

Thanh from C753, the observation soldier who led the counterattack on Hill D, observed they were all crowded together at one end of the Mường Thanh bridge.

A puppet soldier said:

"Lucky you rescued us. It stinks down there ... you terrified us shooting with Stalin's gun!"

I looked at him with hatred and contempt. But I also felt sorry for our nation: how many were brainwashed, divided, and trained to kill each other by the enemy?

As the enemy surrendered, Dakota planes air-dropped supplies. In Hà Nội, Navarre and the puppet army certainly knew about the tragedy and kept sending supplies.

The afternoon light of May 7 began to fade. The sun set behind the mountain range of Upper Laos, bordering China. A few parachutes fell nearby, a box of canned foods broke. We opened a tin box, shared out sweets and biscuits ... young farmer soldiers refused, the *chocolat* was too bitter, and they threw away the cheese.

The fighters armed with 75mm, recoiless guns (DKz), and 120mm greeted each other, boisterous.

The lightly wounded waited for stretchers and were moved to vehicles.

Collapsed tunnels needed urgent repair. Happy about victory but we have to take urgent care of our martyrs, our wounded soldiers, even the enemy wounded in a humanitarian way.

The sky is growing dark. Mines keep exploding!

\

Standing on top of Hill D looking down at Mường Thanh, the whole valley is covered in fog. Flames, thick smoke mixed with parachute fragments, iron walls, and bomb craters, a patchwork of holes, like a huge pile of trash, flickering with fireflies and fen fires ... far to the southwest, the Hồng Cúm ammunition depot[132] in flames goes on exploding in a dazzling halo of fire.

As I watch in situ, I have great admiration for the work, perseverance, courage, and determination of the infantry. Carrying small shovels, they dug trenches from four directions to the center, circling, pushing ... like sharp arrows cutting across the airfield, penetrating under enemy positions.

Wrecks of planes, wings dangling ... perforated steel plates that paved the airstrip, bent and twisted.

Especially Hill A1! The French Africans defended Hill A1 with every possible means ... Suddenly they heard digging sounds from below ... a new level underground.

And then last night, exactly as planned, one single loud "boom!"

I was told that more than half a ton of explosives was detonated! ... with only one sharp sound! An enemy battalion was put out of action!

There were many counterattacks on that fierce hill ... smoke and fire rose up from two burnt-out tanks.

Demolishing Hill A1—the solid shield that barred the way to Route 41 and the Mường Thanh iron bridge—ended our struggle, and opened the way for the General Attack that forced the enemy army and its commander-in-chief to surrender!

Several hundred miles of trenches, perhaps, were dug during this campaign with small shovels! They couldn't dig in the conventional way and use force from above to dig deep into the soil. They dug diagonally ... without raising their arms above their heads, lying on their side, close to the ground, as low as possible to avoid enemy bullets!

In World War I (1914–1918) and World War II (1939–1945), there were endless trenches on both sides of the front line, combat trench number 1, 2, 3 ... During the attacks, fighters saw the enemy formations clearly. Here, in Điện Biên Phủ from the beginning of the siege until just before the final attack, we dug trenches and linked them with the enemy network that led straight to the Central Zone. No longer two sides, only one all together. Gradually, the enemy lost control and could no longer leave their fortifications. They had to gather in groups to counterattack with tank support. That's the bottom line!

I returned to the scene of the Điện Biên Phủ victory. It was getting dark. We found a box of flares and figured out how to use them. Red and blue rays of light flashed in the sky like fireworks … shouting and cheering from the hills. Thanh, the observation soldier, played a tune on his harmonica … On the battlefield, all units were called up to perform new missions.

All went quiet when the curtain of darkness fell. Headlights along Route 41 lit up the Central Zone, General de Castries' command tunnel, and the Mường Thanh Bridge.

Huyến, the political commissar of the C75 mountain artillery, said to Mé from military intelligence:

"Do you know how moved they will be at the rear when they hear the news of this victory?"

"And of the Geneva Conference too?" Mé added.

The crescent moon is tilted. The C753 Command Committee, Cát, Huyến, Phương, Đính, met at the entrance to the bunker. We discussed disarmament and withdrawal. A feast was laid out on a parachute cloth: water jugs, canned food rations from newly parachuted French airdrops, rice balls from our Foster Brother, and notebooks, flashlights.

You can see clearly now: most of the hills around Mường Thanh belong to our battlefields. Hill D was the most unexpected and daring. Hit during the first artillery barrage. From that moment on, every day we stalked each other through loopholes, built into the sandbag walls for observation and snipers.

Soldiers are standing around, hands on each other's shoulders, or sitting down … all are feeling a deep sense of relief.

Someone shouted:

"Hey guys, right now, people on the surrounding high hills are looking down at us! It took us hours to get here on those steep and meandering paths … at least a day's walking!"

The company committee ordered the team in charge of casualty evacuation to leave immediately.

And to organize a group to recover spoils for the artillery.

In the Mường Thanh Valley: people with flashlights, back and forth.

Barbed-wire fence after the war, 1963, signed
Huỳnh Biếc, watercolor on paper, 14 x 25cm.
Collection of the artist.

Infantrymen try out different caliber guns. A mischievous boy pulled the trigger of an enemy 105mm, the shell was in the barrel and exploded, officers reprimanded him. Order to drive two enemy trucks with two new massive heavy artillery guns to the rear ... a lot of artillery in Hồng Cúm.

Infantrymen ran into prostitutes with bobbed curly hair, white powdered faces ... invited soldiers for a drink, they were told off instantly:

"What are you offering? Want to be beaten up!"

Victory and beautiful weather, so cheerful!

Late afternoon sunlight of May 7 over Điện Biên Phủ was unforgettable!

Enemy planes flew over to drop supplies, and no longer dared bomb ... and we had a day to practice pointing our anti-aircraft guns at the sky ... without firing!

Tonight I'm sleeping on top of Hill D, under a sparkling starry sky. It's so quiet ... but inside I feel agitated. I'm looking forward to the morning.

I seemed to be able to forget that every night my whole body had been jolted by enemy artillery shells exploding a few feet away ... when I would realize that I was still alive, I would find the peace to sleep ... and because I was so tired.

May 8, 1954
In the Mường Thanh Valley.

During the fierce fighting and tension of the days waiting ... Time seemed to stand still ...

But today victory has come. I'm in a unique situation: I have access to the Central Zone to see with my own eyes the target of this great battle, this great victory! I'm curious about so many things.

But suddenly I felt time was precious. Command Headquarters called me back. Brothers from all units received orders to clean their guns, get ready to march, bathe, get the mud and dirt off their faces, making up for the times when soil and dirt covered our faces except for our eyes.

We evaluated each other's achievements, wrote down a record of our own exploits during the campaign, and waited for our marching orders.

Remains of planes, tanks, artillery guns crushed by our shells as they hit their targets, mixed with canvas, parachute cords, punctured helmets, and corpses decomposing in muddy trenches with feces, and barbed wire.

Today we gathered the enemy wounded to the center of Điện Biên Phủ for convenient health care. They arrived looking bedraggled, dirty, and ragged—revolting!

Planes flew above and continued to drop supplies for the enemy wounded. We chose what we wanted among the spoils of war. Our soldiers climbed up on enemy tanks. They shouted victory cries that were recorded on film. Truck convoys circulated in daylight. Mines exploded. I heard that Khắc Thịnh, the regiment political commissar, was hit by a mine. Not sure what happened.

Hearing the news of the victory at Điện Biên Phủ (a truly great victory!), we were surprised at first (because it was too sudden) ... Then we cheered and embraced each other ... joyous, jubilant.

❧

Total victory at Điện Biên Phủ.

More than sixteen thousand elite enemy troops were killed and wounded.[133]

Captured[134]: one commanding major general, De Castries; sixteen senior officers; one thousand, seven hundred and forty-nine officers and non-commissioned officers.

Shot down and destroyed sixty-two aircraft.

Seized all depots, weapons, and more than thirty thousand parachutes.

This great victory is unprecedented in the history of the struggle of the Việt Nam People's Army!

❧

Attacks:

First phase: March 13, 1954, peeled the hard shells of Him Lam!

Second phase: March 30, 1954. Hills 1, 2, 3, 4 in the East Zone ... Cang Na Post [French fortification 311] surrendered. The central airport, the South Zone enemy's supply, was cut.

Third phase: May 1, 1954. Four positions in the Central Zone, the headquarters of the South Zone—three hundred meters from the enemy command headquarters.

General Attack: May 6, 1954.

On May 7, 1954, the enemy is forced to surrender.

\\₂

Before leaving for the Điện Biên Phủ Campaign, our unit was stationed in a forest of bamboo and reeds. Someone wrote a poem on bamboo. Sometimes there was a shortage of paper. I transcribed the poem to paper with a Waterman pen. Not sure who the author was. I read it many times to soldiers on marches and during the campaign.

Night in the forest, we camp
Hey soulmate
Do you see the sky?
Full of sparkling gathering stars

Move a little closer
Why are you afraid?
Night dew falls down cold
Protected by a thin blanket

Remember that night, don't you?
Marched the whole night
Breathing hard together
Eyes dreaming of deep sleep
And in the middle of the road, you got a fever
Skinny body, pale skin
Covered in a blanket, shivering
I hold back my tears for you

You recovered: how happy I was!
Share again a poor basket of rice

Drink together a spoonful of water
Your silver [gift], I wear

You have a fried ear of corn
Two of us eat it together
Difficult journeys and hardship
Tighten our friendship …

I look at you so fondly
Hey soulmate
Our homeland was occupied by the enemy
Our families were struggling …

You have a younger sister
Her fragrant, rosy cheeks
Make my heart miss deeply
My old mother in hard times

From villages with bamboo trees and areca fields
To dark misty areas (to military zones dim and immense)
We are all comrades
Standing side by side to fight the common enemy

Sweet and bitter experiences shared
Under the starry night sky we sleep
Embracing each other
Two young soldiers in great friendship.

May 13, 1954
On the road to Tuyên Quang military base (300 miles; ETA by car: 10 hours).

Return to the homeland
Goodbye to "tunnel number one!" In a month and a half, this steep hill

173

will be covered in green vegetation, dense and wild! Oh, the old place, if it hadn't been for the Command Headquarters, nobody would have made the climb!

Before leaving, Foster Brother cooked us a special meal with beef sausages (*món chả bò*, fat, fish sauce, pepper, garlic, and dill) on large banana leaves with wild vegetables, banana flowers, and wild spinach. We had fun decorating the dish and writing with the oily scraps: "CONGRATULATIONS ON OUR VICTORY!"

Some soldiers working in intelligence, mapping, typing, and printing, and in other important roles at headquarters, never went down the mountain to fetch food during the entire campaign. The slope was extremely steep ... they were too busy or lazy. The cooks carried rice and plates up, but the dishes had to be brought back down for the cooks to prepare the next meal! Better go down to the kitchen yourself. There was water to clean your face, hands, and feet ... and don't forget to bring a bamboo container for drinking water, there were no water bottles. By the kitchen, there was a clear stream flowing through shady trees ... enemy planes never discovered it.

On the main road

Vehicles were leaving Điện Biên Phủ during the day, loaded with spoils of war. Soldiers and civic workers from the outskirts poured into the valley ... crowded and noisy. Bits of green parachute in the air. New pairs of shoes thud the ground.

On the road, prisoners carried rice, in ragged, torn clothes, dishevelled. They came here by plane. They're experiencing our soldiers' march. But they should be happy: they're walking on a road in daytime. They don't have to hide in the jungle, worry about hunger, or being attacked [as we did]. And perhaps for the first time they're "equal": White Westerners, Black Westerners, Yellow puppets, low-ranking soldiers, and officers ... all marching together in one long line!

It was a cool morning. The blue mountains were covered in a fog white like snow. Corn is growing in the fields. The countryside seemed greener, brighter, in contrast with the harsh red, black, and grey mountains, hills, and fields of the Điện Biên Phủ Valley where we fought for almost two months.

I met Tháis coming out of the jungle onto the road, following the engineers to get work building roads. Grey-blue smoke rose from the thatched roofs of villages ... villagers have returned. The valley is green with grass and new rice.

A house owner brought his children Sí Pi and Húa Pi to visit their abandoned house. He's planning to build a new one.

Some women civic workers embroidered colorful handkerchiefs for the soldiers.

At a truck stop, I met a performing arts group. They asked the drivers to turn on their headlights and performed for everyone, dancing and singing ... Crowded, fun, an exciting evening. It's been a long time ... so many vehicles pulled up! It was called a car stop but the vehicles carried soldiers, weapons, ammunition, and food ... no passengers. It was a fun place to stop. A shame there were no food stalls or shops!

I met Đông and Long who were going on ahead to prepare a victory meeting for the brigade.

The Tuần Giáo gate [forty-five miles from Điện Biên Phủ] greeted us with a sign:

"Hooray! Điện Biên Phủ victors!"

We could hear the clear voices of children cheering us! People lined the road to watch the soldiers and vehicles go by ...

The Điện Biên Phủ road to Tuần Giáo was beautiful. Straight and newly paved in stone like a gateway ready to welcome everyone to Điện Biên Phủ!

On the Pha Đin Pass

It was raining over the pass ... laborers and Youth Volunteers were covered in nylon (ni-lông), but in good spirits. Some were even fast asleep in the rain.

I was riding with the "weak" and technical brothers—we call them "golden boys"—in charge of paperwork for the great Army's return to headquarters in the Tuyên Quang forest.

Overleaf: Blue mountains and tractor ploughing fields after the war, 1956, watercolor on paper, 26 x 38cm. Collection of the artist.

We're packed in a Molotova truck like watermelons in a field.

"Such a bumpy ride!"

… but I felt good because I don't have to walk on long roads, carrying heavy loads.

Passing Sơn La, I only had time to observe some young men and women building a bridge, shouting. Quickly passed Nà Sản, Hát Lót … stopped in Nà Sản.

May 15, 1954

On the Bản Chẹn Pass[135]

Lines of cars are stuck on the pass. The rains have caused landslides in places. It's easy to understand why our senior officers wanted a victory before the rainy season … Supplies this season had been very difficult.

Hoàng, who was sitting next to me [in the truck], became emotional:

"This road will be the silk road, the sugar road, the salt road. Everyone knows that the people in the Northwest have always lacked salt! The Westerners used to use salt to buy people. People are poor, miserable. Some have large swellings in their throat (goiters)! They burn reeds to lick the salty ash just to get a little salt … and this in a country that has thousands of miles of coastline with so much salt!"

I had butterflies in my stomach. Two-thirds of the road overlooking a precipice had collapsed. Torrents of water flooded across (it was more dangerous than traveling on roads destroyed by enemy bombs). After spending the whole day repairing it, at 11:30 p.m. our truck started moving again!

Further on, a roadside embankment had given way.

"Come on!"

Sounds echoed … Laborers from Thanh Hóa stood in line passing stones to rebuild it. Even fifteen-, sixteen-year-old-boys were working hard. The teenagers had volunteered, they told me. They enjoyed teaming up and competing. By early evening, the embankment had been rebuilt, and the water flowed gently from the upland rice terraces to those below.

What's happening in Điện Biên Phủ right now, I wonder?

I imagine there will be a celebration between soldiers and locals ...
it was a great victory ...

Our soldiers have to clean up the battlefield ... the French Command
Headquarters, Hill A1, Hồng Cúm, Mường Thanh ...

Check how many tanks, heavy artillery, ammunition, warehouses,
and aircraft there are.

Look after the prisoners.

Bury the dead scattered in the trenches and bunkers.

Check the minefields.

Recreate a normal life for the people from the villages in Mường
Thanh, whose life was made miserable by enemy attacks and bombs.

After the liberation, civic workers are continuing to move out of the
area in groups. "Our soldiers are marching back,"[136] to pave the way
for the rebuilding of the Northwest.

Return to Tuyên Quang

Impressions of Peace!

Resistance continues in areas temporarily occupied by the French and
the Vietnamese Army serving the Nguyễn Dynasty. But the atmosphere
is completely different.

"From village to city
Three red flags
Vietnam–China–Soviet Union
And a sea of sky-blue flags[137]
A white dove at the center
... parties, festivals, rallies ... !"

People from the jungle and the high mountains wave flags, smile, sing,
and dance along the road.

Women, children in blue shirts, pink shirts ...

Sweets are selling well, prices have come down.

*Overleaf: Women lay sim flowers on the graves
of the fallen,* 1954, pencil and watercolor on
paper, 26 x 38cm. Collection of the artist.

Children circle around soldiers like birds.

Vehicles are stuck in traffic jams.

Markets are crowded again … they will soon be rebuilt!

New villages are being rebuilt on the old land where they were bombed and destroyed by the enemy.

Every family talks about returning and starting a new life:

"Peace is coming! It's here! No more fear of hunger!"

On the side of the road, a mother asks a soldier:

"Do you know where my son is?"

[I've arrived at the military base in the forest in Tuyên Quang.] After the Victory Celebration in Điện Biên Phủ, I know many of our units are returning to their bases, but haven't arrived yet.

Here in the forest in Tuyên Quang—a beautiful forest with a cool stream winding through it—soldiers are back from the front. They are repairing old shelters and building new camps.

A new meeting hall made of strong bamboo and reeds is being constructed on flat ground, among tall, spacious trees … with chairs and stools made of bamboo. The cook is rounding up pigs and cows, gifts from the province and hamlet committees. He's making preparations to celebrate the success of the Party Congress.

I know the Geneva Conference is taking place, and that a prisoner-of-war exchange is being discussed at the conference.

I feel peace is coming and may be within our reach.

What keeps me focused is that the division/regiment has found white paper, paintbrushes, and colors. All I care about is the communal thatched-roof house I share with my brothers from the propaganda department! We each have a bamboo bed, with four bamboo poles firmly planted in the ground.

A national art exhibition is being held in Hanoi to celebrate the victory. I've started painting.

I have so many things to express I can't express them all! I've finished several watercolors: *Pulling artillery, Artillery shells, Artillery marching up the pass to Điện Biên Phủ, Spring in the artillery bunker of Điện Biên, Artillery shooting at aircraft near Independence Hill, Artillery defending Hill E,*

Infantry attack, and *Civilians building roads and carrying rice*.

I've sent some paintings to the General Command to be considered for the exhibition being organized to celebrate our victory.

August 1, 1954

Happiness! I've been selected to take part in the Hanoi National Exhibition by the arts department of the General Political Office.

August 28, 1954

My heart is mixed with happiness and sadness at leaving my dear companions who stood by me during the Điện Biên Campaign.

I was so moved I was unable to say goodbye when my friends accompanied me to the jungle edge.

Alone with my backpack and rice, I walked down to the plain ... sometimes I feel lonely.

We're in August, autumn has arrived. I'm used to having this feeling when this season comes: is this the autumn we'll go into battle? We often start autumn–winter campaigns!

Phạm Thanh Tâm won third prize at the National Art Exhibition celebrating the Điện Biên Phủ victory in Hanoi. Ten years later, on a day in early autumn, Phạm Thanh Tâm went back to war to report and sketch the American Vietnam War (1964–1975).

Who urges ...
Who urges rice to grow grains
Who urges you to dance to make my heart passionate
Looking at your four-panel traditional dress flying
Pink silk waving and hands softly moving
High voice exchanging love
Oi ... bountiful harvest reaped by skillful hands
Compliments sent to Sam hamlet's girls
Good at growing fragrant rice!
... Hey fragrant grains of rice
You enhance the beauty
Hey the singing girls
You make the village more beautiful!

Our fatherland, our country
Having too much beauty for having too much love ...
Girl, can you fall in love with
The one you met this afternoon?
Poor hamlet since the uprising
Now I have a piece of land, how about a destiny with you?
When I take the buffalo across the path to your house
I keep it there waiting for you to hurry out
When the village communal house has entertainment
Spring afternoons I try to finish work ...
If we have each other
My dear, what love will be more beautiful?
Our love will grow deep to make fields colorful
To firmly hold shovels
As green as the rice seeds you're holding
And as soft as flying pink silk.

Phạm Thanh Tâm, 1954

*Opposite: Barefoot soldier with gun, wearing a piece of
parachute as rain gear,* 1960, signed Huỳnh Biếc,
charcoal on paper, 33 x 24cm. Private collection.

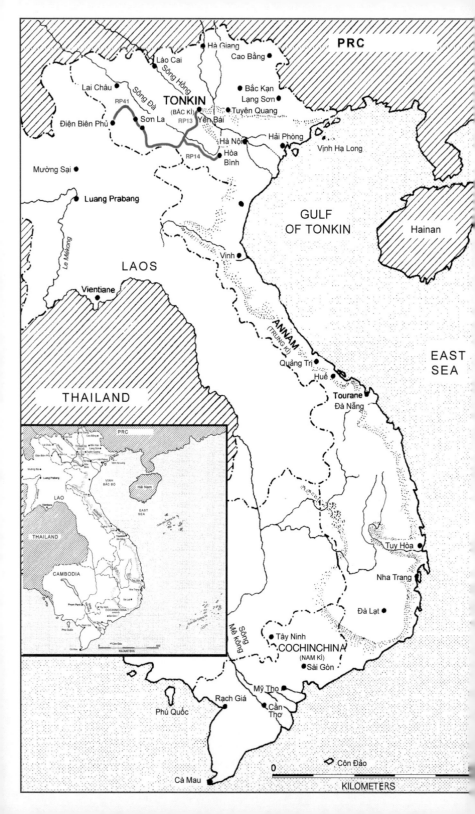

Timeline

French Colonial Rule in Indochina, 1887–1945
1887   French colonial rule begins.
1890   Hồ Chí Minh is born.
1930   Indochina Communist Party is established.

World War II, 1939–1945
1939   World War II begins.
1940   Japan occupies Vietnam.
            The French Vichy government is left in place.
1941   Hồ Chí Minh creates the Việt Minh
            (*Viet Nam Doc Lap Dong Minh*), a communist-led
            nationalist alliance, to fight for Vietnamese independence.
1944   Franco-Japanese-made famine kills an estimated two
            million in the north of Vietnam.

Vietnamese Independence, 1945–1946
1945

March 9   Japanese coup in Vietnam ousts the French.
May 7   German surrender. End of World War II.
August 15   Japanese capitulation.
               The August Revolution.
September 2   Japanese surrender.
               End of World War II in the Pacific.
               Hồ Chí Minh proclaims Vietnamese independence in Hanoi.
               Hồ Chí Minh is the first president of the Democratic
               Republic of Vietnam (DRV).
October 5   French troops land in the south of Vietnam to reclaim their
               colony.

The First Indochina War, 1946–1954
1946   France recognizes Vietnam as a "free state" in the French
               Union.
March 6   French troops land in Haiphong, replacing Chinese troops.

Opposite: 1954 French Map of Indochina.
Tâm's two-hundred-mile itinerary from Yên
Bái to Điện Biên Phủ is in red.

November 23	French warships bombard Haiphong.
December	The Việt Minh set up the Resistance in the Việt Bắc.
	Beginning of the First Indochina War (1946–1954).

1949 — Mao Zedong proclaims the People's Republic of China (PRC).

1950	Creation of the Việt Nam People's Army.
June 26	North Korea invades South Korea.
July 26	The United States sends US$15 million to assist French forces in Vietnam.
September	US Military Assistance Group (MAAG) is established in Saigon to provide secret military aid to the French forces. The PRC supplies the Việt Minh.
October 3–8	The Northwest Campaign.

1951 — The Workers' Party (*Lao động*) is created.

1952 — The Hòa Bình Campaign. French retreat from Hòa Bình.
Dwight D. Eisenhower is elected US president.

1953 — Death of Joseph Stalin.
The Việt Minh launch the Land Reform Program.
Việt Minh offensive in Upper Laos.
General Henri Navarre named commanding officer of the French forces in Indochina.
Navarre Plan sets up an air-defense base at Điện Biên Phủ.
Christian de Castries named commander of the French forces at Điện Biên Phủ.
Hồ Chí Minh and the Politburo decide to attack the French military fortress in Điện Biên Phủ.

The Điện Biên Phủ Campaign, 1954

January 1	Võ Nguyên Giáp named Commander-in-Chief of the People's Army.
January 5	Giáp leaves for the Điện Biên Phủ Campaign.
February 18	The US, UK, France, and the USSR agree to hold a conference in Geneva on Korea and Indochina.
March 13	First phase of the Battle of Điện Biên Phủ.
March 31	Second phase of the Battle of Điện Biên Phủ.
April 26	The Geneva Conference opens.
May 1	Third phase of the Battle of Điện Biên Phủ.
May 7	French capitulation at Điện Biên Phủ.

June 16	Ngô Đình Diệm appointed Prime Minister of the Republic of Vietnam by Emperor Bảo Đại.
July 20	The Geneva Accords provisionally divide Vietnam between the communist Democratic Republic of Vietnam (DRV) and the anti-communist Republic of Vietnam pending national elections by 1956.
October 11	The People's Army enters Hanoi. The United States pledges US$100 million in aid to support Diệm in South Vietnam.

Inter-war Period, 1955–1964

1955	Diệm backed by the United States rejects the Geneva Accords and refuses to participate in nationwide elections.
1959	The Hanoi Politburo adopts Resolution 15 to support the Việt Minh fighting against the Saigon government.
1960	Hồ Chí Minh and the Politburo create the National Liberation Front for South Vietnam.

The American Vietnam War, 1964–1975

1964	Gulf of Tonkin incident.
1965	The United States launches a sustained bombing campaign against the DRV. US Marines land in Da Nang, Republic of Vietnam.
1973	Paris Peace Agreements.
1975	Fall/Liberation of Saigon.

Peace and Reunification, 1975–

| 2024 | Seventieth anniversary of the victory of Điện Biên Phủ. |

Sources: Võ Nguyên Giáp (General), *Điện Biên Phủ: Rendezvous with History*, Hanoi: Thế Giới, 2004; Windrow, Martin, *The Last Valley: Điện Biên Phủ and the French Defeat in Vietnam*, Weidenfeld & Nicolson, 2004; Dalloz, Jacques, *The War in Indo-China, 1945–1954*, Rowman & Littlefield, 1990.

Editor and publisher Sherry Buchanan
presents a copy of the 2005 English-
language edition of *Drawing Under Fire*
to General Võ Nguyên Giáp, Hanoi 2006.

190

Notes

Organization of the Việt Nam People's Army (Quân đội nhân dân Việt Nam)
Division, F, *đại đoàn*
Regiment, E, *trung đoàn*
Battalion, D, *tiểu đoàn*
Company, C, *đại đội*
Section, B, *trung đội*
Squadron, A, *tiểu đội*
Battery, K, *khẩu đội*

The notes are compiled from Sherry Buchanan's interviews with Phạm Thanh Tâm in 2002, 2004, and 2015, and from designated published sources.

On the Road

1   **Ngọc Pier** (*bến*): strategic crossing on the River Chảy in the province of Yên Bái. The French Tactical Air Command (GATAC or Groupement Aérien Tactique) targeted the pier repeatedly to disrupt the People's Army supply route to Điện Biên Phủ.

2   **Engineer-Artillery Division 351**: Phạm Thanh Tâm was a reporter with the newspaper of the Engineer-Artillery Division (*đại đoàn*) of the Việt Nam People's Army, referred to here as the Artillery Division. He traveled with a performing arts group of artists, writers, musicians, singers, and actors. Their job was to entertain the troops and boost morale.

   Võ Nguyên Giáp (General), *Điện Biên Phủ: Rendezvous with History* (Hanoi: Thế Giới , 2004), 467: "Engineer-Artillery Division 351: Artillery Regiment 45 (twenty-four 105mm Howitzers); Engineer Regiment 151; Heavy Weapons Regiment 237 (forty 82mm mortars); Artillery Regiment 675 (fifteen 75mm pack Howitzers and twenty 120mm mortars); Anti-Aircraft Regiment 367 (twenty 37mm AA guns); Field Rocket Unit (twelve to sixteen Katyusha rocket launchers)."

   Giáp, *ibid.*, 10: "The French Far East Expeditionary Corps had five hundred and eighty airplanes—fighter bombers, reconnaissance, and transport planes, ten mechanized regiments (tanks), and three hundred and ninety-one ships."

   The People's Army was supplied by the People's Republic of China after Mao's victory in 1949; the French Expeditionary Corps, by the United States.

3   **River Chảy**: river in the north of Vietnam.

4 **Red River** (*Sông Hồng*): seven-hundred-and-forty-five-mile-long river in the north of Vietnam that starts in the Chinese province of Yunnan and flows to the Gulf of Tonkin.

Giáp, *ibid.*, 58 and 59: "Toward the end of December 1953 ... the Politburo chose Điện Biên Phủ as the decisive battle for the Winter-Spring of 1953–1954. It designated the Party Committee for the Battle ... and myself as general secretary of the Party Committee and also as commander-in-chief ... On December 20, 1953, I gave the instructions directly to the command of our Division 351: 'You'll meet many difficulties installing artillery at the front for the first time. Most important of all, you must preserve security and secrecy on the march.' One day after receiving their orders, the artillery and anti-aircraft units started their march."

5 **Yên Bái Province**: mountainous province of the Northwest, and strategic point on the way to Điện Biên Phủ.

6 **Lũng Lô Pass**: high mountain pass on Route 13 that linked the Việt Minh's Resistance base to Route 41 and Điện Biên Phủ.

Giáp, *ibid.*, 80: "Enemy planes struck repeatedly at important sections of road, mostly on the high passes and at ferries. The Lũng Lô Pass ... became huge bomb craters. Flares were dropped all night long onto key locations."

7 **Route 13**: People's Army supply route from the Việt Minh-controlled territory to the French military camp in Điện Biên Phủ. Routes 13 and 41 were prime targets for French bombing raids. They were part of the French colonial road network, the *routes provinciales*.

Martin Windrow, *The Last Valley: Điện Biên Phủ and the French Defeat in Vietnam* (Weidenfeld & Nicolson, 2004), Kindle Edition, 272: "Targets for these [bombing] missions were scattered along the whole supply route from the Việt Bắc, the main resistance area of the Việt Minh, to Tuần Giáo and beyond, but priority was given to RP 13 bis and RP 41, between the Red River crossing at Yên Bái and Điện Biên Phủ ... During the three-month battle of the roads, about five hundred and sixty-eight tons of bombs were dropped on twenty-three targets."

8 **Điện Biên Phủ**: name of the district, town, and valley, eleven miles long by five miles wide, in Lai Châu Province. The site was chosen by General Henri Navarre in 1953 to build a French military fortress, to defend French-occupied Laos and the Red River Delta against the advance of the People's Army. The French high command believed the camp was impregnable. The Việt Minh controlled the area north of Điện Biên Phủ to the Chinese border.

The French military base was defended by eleven thousand men under the command of Colonel Christian de Castries, heavy artillery, air power, and tanks. Two airfields supplied the camp. Fortified outposts were located on hills around the central command post in the valley: to the north, Gabrielle (Độc Lập); to the northeast Béatrice (Him Lam); to the east the Dominiques (Hills D and E) and the Elianes (Hills C and A); five miles to the south Isabelle (Hong Cum); and to the west, Anne-Marie and the Huguettes.

9   **The new road to Điện Biên Phủ is several hundred miles long:**
Giáp, *ibid.*, 80 and 81: "Our people had restored or opened more than two thousand kilometers of tracks including two thousand kilometers suitable for motorized vehicles ... Most streams did not have bridges ... The road workers made secret bridges for the vehicles to pass."

10 **Youth Volunteers:** auxiliary forces of the People's Army, including thousands of young women. They built and repaired roads and bridges, and detonated unexploded bombs to keep the truck convoys moving.
"Sherry Buchanan, Interview with Phạm Thanh Tâm."

11 **Uncle Hồ:** popular form of address for Hồ Chí Minh (1890–1969), founder and leader of the Việt Minh (*Việt Nam Độc lập Đồng minh*), the National Independence Front, and President of the Democratic Republic of Vietnam (DRV). He declared Vietnamese independence on September 2, 1945 and was the first president of the DRV until his death in 1969.

12 **Civic workers:** *dân công* means "labor service." Civilians were mobilized by the Việt Minh to supply the front. "Labor service" was the equivalent of the French colonial *corvée*, or mandatory labor in lieu of tax. Laborers transported rice, salt, food, medicine, fuel, ammunition, and other necessities on foot, by bicycle, by boat, by horse, and by truck.
Nguyễn Văn Quyền (Col.), "Civilians in the Điện Biên Phủ Campaign," *Institute of Military History Online*, April 26, 2024, para 4: "The total number of civilians mobilized to supply the front at Điện Biên Phủ was more than thirty thousand people."

13 **Vĩnh Phúc Province:** province of the Red River Delta, occupied by the French since the 1951 Battle of Vĩnh Yên.

14 **"Old lady" planes:** The C-119 Flying Boxcar was a US military transport aircraft designed to carry cargo, personnel, and mechanized equipment, and to drop cargo and troops by parachute. They were also used as gunships and were equipped with side-firing weapons that could fire up to six thousand rounds per minute per gun. Beginning in 1953, the aircraft was secretly loaned by the CIA to French forces in Indochina for troop support and reconnaissance. The Vietnamese called the aircraft *bà già*, meaning "old lady," because they flew slowly and at low altitude.

15 **Water bamboo pipes:** pipes (*thuốc lào*) used to smoke tobacco made from the dried leaves of a plant high in nicotine content. Pipe-smoking produced a pleasurable feeling of intoxication.

16 **Frog drum:** frogs are considered a delicacy in northern Vietnam. Children hunt them and make small drums from their skin.
"Sherry Buchanan, Interview with Phạm Thanh Tâm."

17 **Black River** (*Sông Đà*): main tributary of the Red River.

18 **Pack bicycle drivers**: civic workers on foot steered reinforced bicycles.

Nguyễn Văn Quyền, *ibid.*, para 6: "Twenty thousand civilian bicycles were mobilized, transporting one-third of the entire campaign's tonnage. Each bicycle initially carried over two hundred pounds. The load was increased to between four hundred and six hundred pounds."

19 **Bắc Giang Province**: province northeast of Hanoi. The distance between Bắc Giang and Yên Bái Province in the Northwest is around a hundred miles.

20 **Thái Nguyên**: province and town in the Việt Bắc, the center of Việt Minh Resistance against the French, where Hồ Chí Minh set up his government after French troops reoccupied Hanoi in 1945, at the end of World War II.

21 **Mèo**: ethnic minority in northern Vietnam, also known as Hmong, allied with the Việt Minh. The Hmong were mainly wet-rice and opium cultivators.

Christian C. Lentz, "Smouldering Embers," in *Cultivating Subjects: Opium and Rule in Post-Colonial Vietnam*, published online by Cambridge University Press, June 22, 2017, para 3: "During the 1953–54 Điện Biên Phủ Campaign, the Democratic Republic of Vietnam had required Hmong peoples to perform labor service (*dân công*), effectively reversing French colonial policy exempting them from *corvée*."

22 **Performing arts ensembles**: Art, music, theater, and dance groups were embedded with People's Army units. Their repertoire varied from the comic to the revolutionary heroic style.

23 **Cò Nòi**: a stunningly beautiful valley and choke point at the crossroads of Routes 13 and 41, repeatedly targeted by the French Air Tactical Command Group. The bombings temporarily closed the road in December 1953, but it was quickly repaired by the People's Army engineer corps.

Giáp, *ibid.*, 82: "This is the fork where RP13 and RP41 join RP6 from Hanoi … airplanes shooting rockets and dropping bombs interrupted the laborers' work. Cò Nòi was a fork everyone on the way to the front had to pass."

24 **Nà Sản**: French military airbase that preceded the airfield at Điện Biên Phủ, abandoned by the French in August 1953.

25 **Sơn La**: town twenty-eight miles from Tuần Giáo. Engineers had been building the road for three months when Tâm traveled through in March.

"Sherry Buchanan, Interview with Phạm Thanh Tâm."

26 **Pha Đin Pass**: a twenty-mile-long mountain pass regularly bombed by the French Air Tactical Command.

Windrow, *ibid.*, 274: The two points "at either end of the Meo Pass [Pha Đin Pass], were attacked by a total of fifty-eight sorties dropping one hundred and thirty-five tons of bombs, which had only temporary effects on motor traffic."

27 **Thái**: ethnic minority in the north of Vietnam, allied with both sides. The Thái dominated the opium trade in Northwest Vietnam. Several battalions of the French Far East Expeditionary Corps were made up of Thái.

28 **Ban**: tree that flowers in spring in Northwest Vietnam. The flowers (*bauhinia variegata*) are a symbol of young love and decorate the sculpted roofs of Thái houses on stilts.

29 **Engineer Regiment**: Regiment 151 was part of the Engineer-Artillery Division 351, and was in charge of building roads and bridges, repairing them after bombing raids, detonating unexploded bombs, and building underground artillery bunkers for the 105mm Howitzer cannons.

30 **B24s, B26s**: heavy bombers supplied by the United States to the French Air Force. B24s, nicknamed "liberator" during World War II, carried a bomb load of four tons, and flew at thirteen thousand feet. B26s had a bomb load capacity of two tons, and dropped butterfly and napalm bombs. They were also equipped with eight heavy machine guns for ground attacks.

31 **Hellcat**: Grumman F6F fighter aircraft supplied by the United States to the French Navy, loaded with five-hundred-pound bombs, and equipped with machine guns fixed to its wings for ground attacks.

32 **Butterfly bomb**: German anti-personnel bomblet used by the Luftwaffe during World War II. The outer shell contained a large number of four-pound bomblets with variable fuses, particularly dangerous for road-building teams. Wounds were either deadly or difficult to treat.

Giáp, *ibid.*, 91: "The enemy dropped butterfly bombs so that both sides of the road became minefields. The butterfly bombs were green and landed in the vegetation so even by day they were hard to see! The engineer soldiers had to push them aside with poles or hurl rocks at them. But were there other butterfly bombs still in the trees? The engineers bravely used long poles to sweep up the bombs and detonate them right on the spot!"

33 **Võ Nguyên Giáp** (1912–2013): first reference by name in the diary of Võ Nguyên Giáp, Commander-in-Chief of the People's Army. He was a founding member of the Việt Minh, and became Minister of the Interior, then Minister of War in Hồ Chí Minh's first 1945 government. When the 1946 Franco-Vietnamese agreement collapsed, he was named President of the Defense Committee of the Việt Minh in charge of the general insurrection. He was promoted to General in 1947, and directed the People's Army campaigns during the Indochina War. From 1960 to 1980, he was Minister of the National Defense of the Democratic Republic of Vietnam and Vice Prime Minister until 1991. He is the author of several books, including *Điện Biên Phủ: Rendezvous with History* (Hanoi: Thế Giới, 2004).

34 **Calm mind**: concept derived from Buddhism and adopted by communist propaganda to describe strength of mind. The author uses the term to describe the strength of character of soldiers and artillerymen under fire. "Sherry Buchanan, Interview with Phạm Thanh Tâm."

35 **One-thousand-pound bombs**:
"Sherry Buchanan, Interview with Phạm Thanh Tâm": "When the bomb

exploded in mid-air, the fragments dispersed and killed large numbers of soldiers on the battlefield."

36 **Route 41**: Tâm marched on Route 41 from Yên Bái Điện Biên Phủ. It was one of the main supply routes that was built and upgraded by the People's Army Engineer Division and was a prime target of French bombing raids.

37 **C804**: 105mm Howitzer artillery company (*đại đội*). The author trained with C804 in Yunnan in China, and had friends among the artillerymen. C804 consisted of four batteries (*khẩu đội*); each battery had one 105mm Howitzer cannon.

"Sherry Buchanan, Interview with Phạm Thanh Tâm."

38 **105mm cannons**: heaviest artillery of the People's Army. A 105mm cannon weighed two tons, a shell, thirty-three pounds.

"Sherry Buchanan, Interview with Phạm Thanh Tâm."

39 **Withdrawal order**:

Giáp, *ibid.*, 111, 112, and 114: "That day I implemented the hardest decision of my entire life as a military commander ... I phoned the artillery units to inform them: The enemy situation has changed. Our determination to destroy Trần Đình (the code name for Điện Biên Phủ in this campaign) remains unchanged. Our plan of attack has changed. I therefore order you as from 17:00 hours today to haul the heavy guns out of position and back to regroupment areas for new preparations. This order must be strictly executed. No explanation can be provided."

40 **Napalm bombs**: the US Joint Chiefs of Staff gave permission to the French Chief of Staff, General Paul Ely, to drop napalm in Điện Biên Phủ on the condition that "no US crews were involved."

"Memorandum by the Chairman of the Joint Chiefs of Staff (Radford) to the President," in ed., Neil H. Petersen, *Foreign Relations of the United States, 1952–1954, Indochina,* Vol. XIII, 1, March 24, 1954: "[General Ely] was given approval to use C–119 transport aircraft to drop napalm provided no US crews were involved."

41 **Political commissar**: appointed by the Party. Political commissars chaired committees and self- and group-criticism meetings, kept up morale with praise and encouragement, supervised relations between troops and local civilians, and monitored officers and men through internal informers. The political commissar's decisions overrode the decision of the combat commander.

Windrow, *ibid.,* 161: "From the few (inevitably censored) accounts we have of life in the ranks of the People's Army, an impression of genuine admiration for the commissar usually emerges."

42 **Straw**: dried rice stems used to thatch village roofs.

43 **Mission in Upper Laos**: January 29 to February 13, 1954.

Vietnam Military Encyclopedia Online Edition, Volume 1: Military History (People's Army Publishing House, 2015), last para: "The 1954 Upper Laos

Campaign exhausted the enemy's strength, diverted their attention from Điện Biên Phủ, and created conditions for the forces to better prepare for the Điện Biên Phủ Campaign."

Giáp, *ibid.*, 122: "We decided to send Infantry Division 308 to Laos as the best way to cope. The arrival of the Steel Division in northern Laos would attract the enemy's aviation and mobile forces and allow us to pull out our artillery [from DBP]. We needed a long period of preparation to shift our general method to 'Steady Attack, Steady Advance.'"

44   **Regiment 675**: mountain artillery regiment of the Engineer-Artillery Division 351, with fifteen 75mm pack Howitzers and twenty 120mm mortars. Giáp, *ibid.*, 467.

45   *Lạng*: Vietnamese measurement. One *lạng* equals 2.75 ounces.

46   **Wild spinach**: plant that grew in abundance in the jungle. It was a common food source for the troops when rice supplies were low.

"Sherry Buchanan, Interview with Phạm Thanh Tâm."

47   **They remained steadfast and stuck to the rules**:

"Sherry Buchanan, Interview with Phạm Thanh Tâm": "On joining the Army, a Việt Minh soldier swore by an honor code which regulated our behavior towards civilians. The rules included not entering a civilian house without being invited, cleaning quarters that had been lived in by soldiers, and only accepting food if the family had enough of their own."

48   **Dakotas**: or Douglas C47s, transportation planes supplied by the United States. During the siege of Điện Biên Phủ, Dakotas were used for the evacuation of the French wounded and for parachuting in paratroopers, food, munitions, and weapons—even 155mm—to the besieged French troops.

Windrow, *ibid.*, 354: "[At Điện Biên Phủ], on some days the Dakotas and C-119 would achieve up to sixty missions."

49   **Tuyên Quang**: military base at the rear, three hundred miles from Điện Biên Phủ on Route 13.

50   **Souphanouvong** (1909–1995): Laotian prince, nicknamed the Red Prince, founder of the Pathet Lao, an anti-colonial party allied with the Việt Minh. His half-brother, Souvanna Phouma, was the founder of the rival party, the Lao Issara.

51   **American pilots**: US pilots worked for CAT, a CIA-owned air fleet. They piloted Dakotas, the transport planes that airlifted and parachuted supplies to the French Expeditionary Corps in Điện Biên Phủ. The American technicians on the ground were US Air Force personnel. The United States was officially not a party to the war, but secretly provided financial and material aid to the French.

"Memorandum for the Record, Meeting of the President's Special Committee on Indochina, January 29, 1951," in ed., Neil H. Petersen, *Foreign Relations of the United States, 1952–1954, Indochina, Vol. XIII, 1*. Department of State, Office of the Historian. S/S-NSC files, lot 63 D 351, NSC 5405 Series: "Summary of Action Agreed Regarding Urgent French Requests. It was agreed: a) To provide a total of 22 B26 aircraft as rapidly as practicable. b) To provide 200 uniformed US Air Force mechanics who would be assigned as an augmentation to MAAG, Indochina. These mechanics to be provided only on the understanding that they would be used at bases where they would be secure from capture and would not be exposed to combat. c) To send the CAT pilots, with CIA arranging necessary negotiations."

52 **"Steady attack, Steady advance."**: General Giáp announced the new battle plan and motto on January 26, 1954, after he took the difficult decision of delaying the offensive until March.

Giáp, *ibid.*, 110: "Given the essential principle of 'attacking with the certainty of victory,' it is imperative that we change our guiding philosophy from 'Fast strike, fast victory' to 'Steady attack, steady advance.'"

53 **Hải Lăng**: code name for Regiment 45, the 105mm Howitzer Artillery Regiment of the Engineer-Artillery Division 351, with "twenty-four 105mm Howitzers." Giáp, *ibid.*, 467.

54 **Long Châu**: code name for the Engineer-Artillery Division 351, Giáp, *ibid.*

55 **Châu Giang**: code name for Regiment 675, the mountain artillery regiment of the Engineer-Artillery Division 351, "with twenty 120mm mortars, and fifteen 75mm mountain artillery guns (pack Howitzers)." Giáp, *ibid.*

56 **Bến Tre**: code name for Infantry Division 312. Bến Tre Province, a rice-growing province in the Mekong Delta in southern Vietnam, was a center of the resistance to French colonial rule.

57 **Artillery bunkers:** built by People's Army engineers, artillerymen, and infantrymen for the 105mm Howitzers.

Giáp, *ibid.*, 154–155: "Building shelters for the heavy guns required additional work. The crews fitted these shelters deep inside the mountains. These bunkers had their own fortifications for firing and for cover yet allowed the gunners to move about easily during a fight. The shelters had covers that were three meters (ten feet) of wood and earth mixed with bamboo … Each gun shelter required digging from 200 to 300 cubic meters of earth and rock, which were then thrown on top of the shelter for the roof. Roofing timbers had diameters of about thirty centimeters. Troops hauled all the wood from sites nine to ten kilometers away in order not to reveal the gun emplacements. This was an enormous volume of work!"

Windrow, *ibid.*, 291–292: "The People's Army artillery positioned in well-constructed casemates was so well camouflaged it was not detected by the French prior to the battle."

In the Trenches

58 **Coordinated attack:**
   Điện Biên Phủ Historical Victory Museum, "Artillery Regiment 351 in the Điện Biên Campaign," *The People's Army Newspaper Online,* April 23, 2024, last para: "The role of Artillery Group F351 in this battle is extremely important ... For the first time, we advocated a coordinated attack between the artillery and infantry. The artillery was mobilized at the highest level to provide maximum fire power for infantry units."
   Giáp, *ibid.,* 203: "We had four requirements for a victorious campaign ...[One requirement was to] Ensure close coordination [between artillery and infantry]."

59 **Him Lam:** the first French stronghold to be occupied by the People's Army.

60 **Độc Lập:** the northernmost French fortification. A French counter-attack on March 15 failed.

61 **Anti-aircraft guns** (*pháo cao xạ*): cannons characterized by a very long tube. A French–US report concluded before the battle that the anti-aircraft guns would be easily destroyed by French fighter bombers because the long tubes were too difficult to camouflage.
   Trần Liên, "Điện Biên Phủ Campaign: Anti-aircraft artillery and a surprise blow to the enemy," *dantri.com.vn,* April 29, 2024.

62 **75mm mountain cannon** (*son phao*): pack Howitzers, lighter than 105mm Howitzers and 120mm mortars. The cannon could be dismantled into separate parts and carried up hills, making it easier and faster to move than the 105mm cannons. It also fired at a steeper angle than the 105mm. The disadvantage was that 75mm pack Howitzers could not be hidden in underground shelters, making artillerymen particularly vulnerable to enemy fire.
   Windrow, *ibid.,* 152: "... reportedly US light 75mm pack Howitzers captured from Chinese nationalists."

63 **120mm mortar** (*co phao*): Soviet mortar with a shorter range than the 105mm Howitzer but almost as powerful.

64 **C805:** part of Artillery Regiment 45, the 105mm Howitzer heavy artillery company with four batteries. Giáp, *ibid.,* 647.

65 **"Hold onto your Youth":** poem sent by a guerrilla fighter at the rear to her older brother at Điện Biên Phủ and published in the front line *People's Army Newspaper* on March 10, 1954.
   The People's Army Newspaper, May 3, 2014: "The younger sister was worried about her brother on the battlefield who could not stand the difficulties and hardships. She sent him a poem to remind him of their family torn apart by French colonial rule, and encourage him to fight, and take revenge."

66 **C757:** Anti-aircraft artillery company.

67 **Mường Thanh:** People's Army designation for the French headquarters at

Điện Biên Phủ. It was the name of the Thái village displaced by the French troops to set up their camp. In 1953, General Navarre chose the valley of Điện Biên Phủ as the site for their new air-defense base and occupied Mường Thanh. Under French rule, the area had been a center of the opium trade.

68 **Pathet Lao:** Laotian communist party allied with the Việt Minh.

69 **Uncle Hô's Letter:** President Hồ Chí Minh, "Letter to officers and soldiers at the Điện Biên Phủ front, March 14, 1954," facsimile reproduced in *The People's Army Newspaper Online,* May 7, 2024, and Giáp, *ibid.,* 206.

70 **Phạm Ngọc Mậu** (1919–1993): general of the People's Army. During the Điện Biên Phủ Campaign, he was the political commissar of the Engineer-Artillery Division 351. His real name was Phạm Ngọc Quyết. https://vi.wikipedia.org/wiki/Ph%E1%BA%A1m_Ng%E1%BB%8Dc_M%E1%BA%ADu
Giáp, *ibid.,* 467.

71 **Targets in the East:**
Điện Biên Phủ Historical Victory Museum, "Artillery Regiment 351 in the Điện Biên Campaign," *The People's Army Newspaper Online,* April 23, 2024: "Him Lam (Béatrice); Hill E (Dominique 1); Hill D (Dominique 2); Hill D2 (Dominique 3); and Hills A1 and C1 (Elianes)."

72 **Battalion 954:** 105mm Howitzer artillery battalion (*tiểu đoàn*) made up of companies (*đại đội*) C801, C802, C803 with a total of twelve 105mm cannons. A company consisted of four batteries. Each battery had one 105mm Howitzer.

73 **The entire regiment opens fire:** Artillery Regiment 45 with twenty-four 105mm Howitzers; included companies 801, 802, 803, 804, 805, and 806.
Giáp, *ibid.,* 467.

74 **Fake battlefield:** People's Army subterfuge to attract French artillery fire onto false artillery positions. Artillerymen positioned by the wooden cannons set off explosions to simulate the smoke effect of artillery fire.

75 **Helicopter:** the French Combined Army Helicopter Unit (GHFAT) evacuated the seriously wounded to Muong Sai, a French airbase in Upper Laos.
Windrow, *ibid.,* 30: "The helicopters' range limited them to running a shuttle service for casualties to Muong Sai."

76 **Position 201:** possibly Eliane 10.
Windrow, *ibid.,* 376: "Under cover of night on March 12, three of (the 155mm) had been towed forward to pits east of the river in location Eliane 10, less open to enemy observation. The late move to Eliane 10 had not been spotted by the Việt Minh."

77 **Foot of one of the D Hills:** Hill D, French stronghold Dominique, was made up of several hills. Six heavy mortars on Hill D supported the French artillery on Him Lam (Béatrice), the hill targeted on March 13. The 105mm French batteries positioned on Hill D2 (Dominique 3) resisted until May 2, 1954.

78 **Regiments 209** and **141** or **149:** infantry regiments of the Bến Tre infantry division 312.

Windrow, *ibid.*, 379: "At about 3 p.m. on March 13, Regiments 141 and 209—inspired by an order of the day from President Hồ Chí Minh—left their forming-up areas in thick forests and moved forward to their jumping-off points. By this time three trenches had already been pushed to within about 50 yards of the wire, hidden by scrub; one of the RCL positions was within 100 yards of Béatrice 1 (Him Lam)."

79 **Subjective:** from the Vietnamese *chủ quan.* The word in the diary has a negative connotation and signifies pessimistic, complacent, careless, arrogant. The opposite, objective (*khách quan*), denotes a positive, optimistic attitude.

80 **Three enemy stations were attacked:** French fortified posts on Him Lam Hill. All French posts on Him Lam were overrun by the People's Army Infantry Regiments 209 and 141 during the first phase of the People's Army offensive on March 13.

81 **All stations on Him Lam were resolved at half past midnight:** the fall of Him Lam allowed the People's Army to move their artillery forward to positions closer to the French central command post. During the first general offensive, the People's Army also seized the French stronghold Gabrielle (Độc Lập), the northernmost French fortification. A counterattack against Độc Lập by the French failed on March 15.

82 *Căm thụ:* Tâm uses the term hate or vengeance several times in the diary to describe the rallying cries of Việt Minh soldiers before going into battle. Việt Minh war propaganda encouraged feelings of revenge against French colonial crimes: arbitrary detention, systemic torture and rape in colonial jails, extra-judicial killings during raids on villages, indiscriminate bombardments that resulted in civilian deaths, and the man-made famine that killed an estimated two million people during the French-administered Japanese occupation between 1944 and the summer of 1945. The great famine rallied popular support for the Việt Minh.

83 **Hill E:** French stronghold Dominique 1.

84 **Hòa Bình Campaign:** Hòa Bình was a strategically important town and province southwest of Hanoi. The Battle of Hòa Bình took place between November 10 and February 25, 1952, and ended in victory for the People's Army. Both sides suffered heavy casualties.

85 **C119:** 105mm Howitzer company renamed Company 806, and merged into Regiment 45. The company participated in the 1952 Hòa Bình Campaign. Tâm writes: "They were first posted with C124 and then sent to C119 in Đức Ký. Comrade Đệ was the leader, Cao Đoán was the political instructor."

Nguyễn Tất Lộc, "Meeting the Former Artilleryman Again and the First Rounds of Bullets Fired at Him Lam to open the Điện Biên Phủ Campaign," *baoxaydung.com.vn online*, March 26, 2014, para 4: "These were the first gunners of the Việt Nam People's Army to use heavy artillery to destroy French troops and vehicles [during the 1952 Hòa Bình Campaign]."

86 **Thất Khê**: one of several French military bases, forts, and defensive posts along the Chinese border captured by the People's Army during the 1950 Border Campaign.

Giap, quoted in Nguyễn Văn Mai, "Battle of acupuncture points in Đông Khê and Thất Khê," *The People's Army Newspaper Online,* November 6, 2011: "Attack Đông Khê and Thất Khê is to attack one place, if that place is destroyed, the other two will still be won without fighting. Losing Đông Khê and Thất Khê, the enemy in Cao Bằng and Lang Son will have to flee because there is no more supply route … The evacuating French troops left behind 13 cannons, 120 mortars, 450 vehicles, 240 machine guns, 850 rifles, 10,000 shells and 130,000 gallons of petrol."

87 **Đông Khê**: French defensive post along the Chinese border captured by the People's Army during the 1950 Border Campaign.

88 **Cao Bằng**: French defensive post along the Chinese border captured by the People's Army during the 1950 Border Campaign.

89 **Tết**: Lunar or Chinese New Year, usually in February, the beginning of the dry season in northern Vietnam, and chosen by the People's Army for their winter campaigns.

90 **Thục Luyện**: a town twenty-five miles north of Hòa Bình.

91 **Leftover ammunition**: shortages of ammunition were common.

92 **Enemy thought our infantry was attacking, so they dispersed, and ran**: Bernard B. Fall, *Street Without Joy,* Stackpole Military History, Kindle Edition 2018, 89: "… the French once more had been the heavier losers, for while the Việt Minh used the battle for the Black River salient as a sort of dress rehearsal for a future showdown battle, the French apparently failed to consider the operation as either a dress rehearsal or as a portent of things to come."

93 **Ba Vành**: French fortified camp near Hòa Bình captured by the People's Army during the Battle of Hòa Bình.

94 **Phú Thọ**: province that was a gateway to the Việt Bắc Resistance base. During the 1952 Northwest Campaign, after several battles the French forces withdrew from Phú Thọ on November 25, 1952.

95 **Hồng Cúm**: French stronghold five miles south of the central headquarters, with a second airfield that resisted until the French capitulation on May 7.

96 **Charles Jean Clément Piroth** (1906–1954): French artillery officer and World War II veteran. Piroth commanded the artillery during the Battle of Điện Biên Phủ. He was bold and optimistic before hostilities erupted, exulting: "I've got more guns than I need." After failures by his artillery batteries to provide adequate support, he committed suicide in his bunker. https://en.wikipedia.org/wiki/Charles_Piroth

Giáp, *ibid.,* 155: "The careful preparatory work for our artillery positions would plunge the French artillery commander at Điện Biên Phủ into such utter despair that soon after the battle began he killed himself with a grenade."

Windrow, *ibid.*, 412: "The one-armed artilleryman had tormented himself with his failure since the evening of March 13—Castries had already asked a chaplain to keep an eye on him; now he took his shame to the privacy of his quarters; at some time on March 15, Piroth took a grenade in his one hand, pulled the pin with his teeth, and clutched it to his chest."

97 **Bản Kéo**: reference to the Battle of Bản Kéo, or the Bản Kéo Mutiny, the final major event in phase 1 of the Điện Biên Phủ Campaign. The event took place on March 17. Soldiers from a Thái battalion defending Bản Kéo Hill (Anne-Marie 1 and 2) deserted en masse, allowing the People's Army to capture the Anne-Marie base without having to fire a shot. Vietnamese ethnic minorities fighting on the French side (*ngụy binh*) made up twenty percent of the French forces.

Giáp, *ibid.*, 237: "Even enemy cannon fire couldn't stop the Thái soldiers! Our artillery rained down on the enemy artillery positions in support of the the Thái soldiers running toward safety in the forest. [We] didn't need to fire a single round to capture Anne-Marie 1 and 2. Now we controlled all the hilltops north of the airport."

98 **Tố Hữu** (1920–2002): official poet of the Communist Party and cultural czar named Deputy Cultural Minister in 1955. One of his most famous poems was a eulogy to Stalin, written on the occasion of the death of the Soviet leader.

99 **General Henri Navarre** (1898–1983): French Army general and seventh and final commander of the French Far East Expeditionary Corps. The Navarre Plan was to build entrenched camps such as Điện Biên Phủ in anticipation of an international negotiated settlement in Indochina. https://en.wikipedia.org/wiki/Henri_Navarre

100 **General René Cogny** (1904–1968): French General, World War II, French Resistance veteran, and survivor of Buchenwald and Mauthausen-Gusen concentration camps. He was a commander of the French forces in Tonkin (northern Vietnam) during the Battle of Điện Biên Phủ.

101 **Nguyễn Văn Tâm** (1893–1990): head of the French-installed Saigon government in 1952, he had been Minister of the Interior and Governor of North Vietnam during French colonial rule.

102 **American Advisor**: Lieutenant General John W. ("Iron Mike") O'Daniel was the head of the US Military Assistance Advisory Group (MAAG) based in Saigon. MAAG was created in August 1950 to disburse military and economic aid—estimated at US$ 2.6 billion or eighty percent of the French war effort, to the French Expeditionary Corps and provide them with technical expertise. The first US shipment of F6F Hellcat fighter bombers under the Mutual Defense Assistance Program was made in October 1950. A number of American advisors, including O'Daniel, made several visits to Điện Biên Phủ.

Richard W. Stewart, *The US Army Campaigns for the Vietnam War: Deepening Involvement 1945–1965*, Center of Military History, US Army, 2012,

14: "General O'Daniel inspected the Điện Biên Phủ outpost in February 1954 and left encouraged by the overall impression of French strength."

103 **The Vietnamese Workers' Party** (*Đảng Lao động Việt Nam,* DLDVN): created in 1951 to replace the Communist Party which had been dissolved in 1945 to attract nationalist factions to the Việt Minh.

104 **Stalingrad**: Soviet city besieged by Hitler's forces during World War II from August 19, 1942 until January 27, 1943. The Soviet Red Army defeated the Nazis with a huge cost to human life. Điện Biên Phủ has been compared to the Battle of Stalingrad and called the Stalingrad of the East.

105 *Mô-lô-tô-va*: Soviet-supplied truck used to tow the 105mm Howitzers and transport ammunition. Six hundred Soviet trucks, each weighing five hundred and fifty pounds, transported weapons, ammunitions, and supplies of the People's Army to Điện Biên Phủ. The troops usually marched.

106 **Land Reform**: Workers' Party program "to give the land to those who work the land" that affected an estimated two million people. The program encouraged hundreds of thousands to join the Việt Minh. Việt Minh fighters and their families were given priority for land. The first Land Rent Reduction Campaign was introduced in 1953 before the Điện Biên Phủ Campaign, the second campaign, after the 1954 victory (1954–1956). The Land Reform Program was a success at first, but led to the excessive repression and the arbitrary extra-judicial killings of an estimated thirteen thousand landlords in North Vietnam. In August 1956, DRV president Hồ Chí Minh apologized and acknowledged the serious errors the government had made during the Land Reform Program. The program was discontinued.

   William Duiker, *Hồ Chí Minh: A Life*: "After planning the Điện Biên Phủ campaign, Party leaders decided to strengthen the Land Reform Program to win support from poor peasants."

107 **Geneva Conference**: The four great powers met in Berlin on February 18, 1954 to set a date for the Geneva Conference to settle the conflicts in Korea and Indochina. The participation of a Việt Minh delegate, opposed at first by France and the United States, was backed by the Soviet Union.

108 **Nậm Rốm**: river flowing through the valley of Điện Biên Phủ. The French headquarters and central camp were on the western bank of the river; the People's Army positions were on the eastern bank. An iron bridge known as the Bailey bridge and a wooden foot bridge connected the two banks.

109 **Trường Chinh** (1907–1988): member of the Politburo during the Điện Biên Phủ Campaign and General Secretary of the Vietnamese Workers' Party (DLDVN). He was the Party's theoretician and author of *We Will Win* (1947), a practical guide on revolutionary guerrilla warfare, read by new recruits in Việt Minh training camps.

110 **Hill D**: French defense post occupied after March 30 during phase two.

111 **Hill A1**: strongest French defense post, made up of several hills. The People's

Army attacked Hill A1 (Eliane 2) during the second phase, along with Hills E, D, and C1 (Eliane 1). The People's Army captured Hills E and D, but Hill A1 resisted until May 7, when a Việt Minh commando dynamited the French command post from a tunnel.

"April 3, 1954: Handing Over the Battlefield on the Eastern Slope of Hill A1 and Using Forces to Attack Base 105," *Nhân Dân Newspaper Online*, April 3, 2024: "General Võ Nguyên Giáp ordered the units to "temporarily stop fighting from April 4 and maintain the captured position on Hill A1 to continue attacking when ordered." Vietnam had not yet completed all the set goals, especially since we had not captured Hill A1—a key goal of this attack."

112 **Hill C1**: the People's Army attacked Hill C1 during the second phase of the campaign on the night of March 31. The French counterattacked with battalions, artillery, tanks, and fighter planes on April 10 and 11, and reoccupied the position until May 1 when it was overrun by the People's Army.

113 **Tank**: The United States supplied the French garrison at Điện Biên Phủ with M24 Chaffee tanks. The light tanks were disassembled, parachuted into Điện Biên Phủ, and used in infantry support missions. The People's Army did not have any tanks.

Windrow, *ibid.*, 306: "Ten M24 tanks Chaffee, weighing each eighteen tons, were parachuted into Điện Biên Phủ."

114 **Hill E1**: The People's Army artillery and infantry overran Hill E (Dominique 1 and 2) on March 30, at the same time as Hill D. The mountain artillery was positioned on Hill E1 to defend it against French counterattacks.

115 **Tấu Village**: Thái village in the Điện Biên Phủ valley, north of Độc Lập Hill, destroyed by enemy bombings.

116 **Hải Dương**: a province in the Red River Delta under French occupation.

117 *Sim* **flowers:** Myrtle flowers were traditionally left by young girls on the tombs of their loved ones killed in war.

118 **Limits to our success**: blamed on "a rightist tendency" during the second phase of the campaign among high-ranking officers who doubted that victory was possible. The Political Bureau instructed the Party committees to suppress all "subjective" tendency through self- and group-criticism sessions, from the division level down to individual combat units.

Giáp, *ibid.*, 5th edition, 1994, 130, quoted in Kevin Boylen, *Valley of the Shadow: The Siege of Dien Bien Phu* (Osprey Publishing, 2018): "A negative tendency appeared among some of our officers and men, in various forms: fear of casualties, losses, difficulties, and hardships, as well as fatigue, underestimation of the enemy, subjectivism, and self-conceit."

119 **Vyacheslav Molotov** (1890–1986): Minister of Foreign Affairs of the USSR and delegate to the Geneva Conference. Molotov is credited for having convinced France and the United States to include a Việt Minh delegate at the Geneva Conference, after their initial opposition.

Foreign Relations of the United States, 1952–1954, The Geneva Conference,
Volume XVI, 396.1 GE/4–754 Memorandum Prepared in the Department of
State secret [Washington], April 7, 1954, Terms of Reference for the Paris
Working Group on Indochina Phase at Geneva: "… our [the US] position on
participation so far is definite only for the US, UK, France, USSR, Communist
China, Vietnam, Cambodia, and Laos, and our position on further participants
[such as Hồ Chí Minh] is not yet firm."

120 **155mm**: French heavy artillery.

Dominique Lemaire, *Encyclopédie des cannons de la deuxième guerre mondiale:*
"The four 155mm cannons at Điện Biên Phủ had a longer firing range of
nine miles than the 105mm and their shells were more destructive. They were
air transported to Điện Biên Phủ by Dakota transport planes."

121 **Colonel Christian Marie Ferdinand de la Croix de Castries** (1902–1991):
French Commanding Officer at the Battle of Điện Biên Phủ. He was born into
a distinguished military family, and enlisted in the army at the age of nineteen.
After Điện Biên Phủ, he was held prisoner for four months. He retired from
the military in 1959 after a car accident.

122 **Infantry Regiment 176**: the regiment was incomplete. Giáp, *ibid.*, 466.

123 **Tu Vũ**: military fortress of the French Far East Expeditionary Corps on the
Black River, and site of a battle during the 1952 Hòa Bình Campaign.

124 **Three-men teams** (*tam tam chế*):

Windrow, *ibid.*, 159: "They (the political commissars) tried to follow the
Chinese model of internal surveillance: each platoon was divided for tactical
purposes into teams of three men or *tam tam chế*, and one of these soldiers—
whose identity was kept secret—was also supposed to be a Party member,
tasked with both encouraging and spying on his comrades."

125 **Phùng Văn Khầu** (1930–2021): colonel and Hero of the People's Army. During
the Battle of Điện Biên Phủ, on March 30, 1954, his unit destroyed enemy
bunkers on Hill E1. On April 2, the unit positioned three mountain artillery
guns on Hill E1 to support the infantry attacks. On April 23, the French
launched a major counterattack to retake E1 Hill. French fire power destroyed
the camouflage bunkers of two 75mm mountain artillery guns. Eighteen of
his comrades died and were wounded, leaving only one of his batteries to
fight.

Giáp, *ibid.*, 303: "Phùng Văn Khầu aimed his gun and pulled the trigger,
silencing four 105mm enemy guns in only ten minutes. His detachment
held that volcano for thirty-six days and nights, constantly threatening
enemy positions in the plain. What a pity our guns became shell-hungry!
We had to transfer gunners to other duties."

126 **Bunkers**: 75mm guns had a higher elevation angle than 105mm Howitzers.
They were positioned in open shallow gun pits with no cover. This gave the
artillerymen a wider firing range but less protection than the underground

artillery bunkers built for 105mm cannons.

127 **Japanese gun**: the 75mm 94 series weighed half a ton with a projectile weighing thirteen pounds. It was one of the cannons that was probably seized by the People's Army at the end of World War II when the Japanese surrendered to the Allied forces in Indochina. Unlike the 105mm, this cannon was built for mountainous terrain and could be dismantled into separate parts and carried. "Sherry Buchanan, Interview with Phạm Thanh Tâm."

128 **American gun**: artillerymen and infantrymen of the People's Army dragged two hundred cannons through mountain passes and over hills, including twenty-four 105mm Howitzers of US manufacture, which had been captured in Korea by the People's Liberation Army of the People's Republic of China.

Going Home

129 **Katyusha**: rocket launcher developed by the Soviets towards the end of the World War II, nicknamed "Stalin's organs" by the German troops, who likened the thundering noise of its firing power to the sound of a church organ.

Giáp, *ibid.*,467: "[Our] Field rocket unit had twelve to sixteen Katyusha rocket launchers."

130 **White flags from parachute fabric**: the French High Command in Hanoi did not want a capitulation with an official white flag. According to Tâm, French soldiers emerged from their undergrounds waving white pieces of cloth. Recently digitized photographs from French and Vietnamese national archives confirm Tâm's account.

Photo, Ministère des Affaires étrangères/CVN, with the caption: "*Les soldats français hissant le drapeau blanc pour se rendre en 1954.*" "French soldiers raise the white flag to surrender in 1954."

Center of National Archives Number 3, Hanoi, "La Victoire de Diên Biên Phu dans les archives: Les archives sur la Campagne de Diên Biên Phu et la Conférence de Genève de 1954 sont conservées en bon état au Centre national d'archives N°3, à Hanoï," May 5, 2024. https://lecourrier.vn/la-victoire-de-dien-bien-phu-dans-les-archives/1231258.html

131 **Command Headquarters**: General Giáp's command post in the jungle thirty-nine miles northeast of Mường Thanh on Route 41.

132 **Hồng Cúm ammunition depot**: the French blew up their own munitions depot in Hồng Cúm so it wouldn't fall into enemy hands after the capitulation of their forces on May 7.

133 **Killed and wounded**: French sources estimate that three thousand of their troops were killed and five thousand were wounded.

Vietnam published the official number of Vietnamese casualties at the Battle of Diên Biên Phu in 2018.

Vietnam Television (VTV), "Điện Biên Phủ Victory and Numbers," *Việt Nam TV Online*, May 7, 2018: "Our troops sacrificed four thousand and twenty people, seven hundred and ninety-two people are missing, and nine thousand, one hundred and eighteen people were injured."

134 **Captured**: The Việt Minh were accused of mistreating POWs and blamed for the high death rate amongst the prisoners. Vietnamese sources and recent French sources counter-argue that POWs received humane treatment, were housed in jungle camps in conditions equal to those of the Vietnamese population around them, and given equal food rations.

Nguyễn Hữu Đông (Kỳ Thu), "Điện Biên Phủ Prisoners of War are Grateful to Uncle Hồ's Soldiers," *Nhân Dân*, May 9, 2024; and, Thanh Hương, "French Prisoners of War at Điện Biên Phủ: Vietnam's Lenient Policy Has Awakened Us," *The People's Army Newspaper*, qdnd.vn online, April 28, 2024.

Julien Mary, "Les prisonniers français au Vietnam," *Chemin de Mémoires*, Ministère des armées: "In the camps improvised by the DRV, overwhelmed by numbers, [POWs] were subjected to a food and health regime which, if close to that of the Vietnamese populations surrounding them, wreaked havoc in the ranks of Europeans and Africans, particularly in the camps of non-commissioned officers and enlisted men." https://www.cheminsdememoire. gouv.fr/fr/revue/les-prisonniers-francais-au-vietnam

135 **Bản Chẹn Pass**: mountain pass at the strategic intersection of supply Routes 13 and 41, targeted by French bombings to cut supplies to Điện Biên Phủ.

136 **"Our soldiers marching back"**: lyric from *The Liberation of Điện Biên*, a well-known revolutionary song by Đỗ Nhuận (1922–1991). Đỗ Nhuận was the composer of numerous patriotic songs during the First Indochina War (1946–1954). After the war, he became an acclaimed composer of classical Vietnamese operas.

137 **The United Nations flag**: The flag was created in 1949. The Việt Minh adopted the flag for festivities and celebrations. The white dove in the center, modeled on a Picasso drawing, was a symbol of peace and harmony between nations.

Select Bibliography

NOTE: The spellings of Dien Bien Phu vary and are faithful to how they appear in printed versions of the books listed below.
Vietnamese-language publications: Điện Biên Phủ
English-language publications: Dien Bien Phu
French-language publications: Diên Biên Phu

Art During the Vietnam Wars, 1946–1975

BUCHANAN, SHERRY.
   On The Ho Chi Minh Trail: The Blood Road, The Women Who Defended It, The Legacy. London: Asia Ink, 2021.
   "A History of Posters in the Socialist Republic of Vietnam," *Communist Posters.* London: Reaktion, 2017.
   Vietnam Posters. London: Prestel, 2009.
   Mekong Diaries: War Artists' Drawings & Stories. Chicago: The University of Chicago Press, 2008.
   Vietnam Zippos: American Soldiers' Engravings & Stories. Chicago: The University of Chicago Press, 2007.
   "Artists and the Role of Propaganda," *Vietnam Behind the Lines: Images from the War, 1965–1975.* London: British Museum Press, 2002.
   "Drawing Fire," *The Guardian,* June 10, 2002.
   "Silent Warrior," *The Independent on Sunday,* June 2002.
   Tran Trung Tin: Paintings and poems from Vietnam. London: Asia Ink and Thames & Hudson, 2001.
   "Rebel with a Cause: The Violent Past of Southeast Asia Still Haunts Artists and Their Work," *Asian Art News,* May/June 1996.
   "Buu Chi: Bittersweet Hope of a Vietnamese Artist," *The International Herald Tribune,* November 25, 1994.
BÙI THANH PHƯƠNG and TRẦN HẬU TUẤN. *Bùi Xuân Phái: Life and Work.* Hanoi, 1999.
CLARK, TOBY. *Art and Propaganda in the Twentieth Century.* London, 1997.
FAST, HORST and PAGE, TIM. *Requiem: Photographers Who Died in Vietnam and Indochina.* Random House, 1997.
HARRISON-HALL, JESSICA and BUCHANAN, SHERRY. "The Unseen War," *British Museum Magazine,* Summer 2002.
HARRISON-HALL, JESSICA with BUCHANAN, SHERRY, and STERN, THU. *Vietnam Behind the Lines: Images from the War, 1965–1975.* London: The British Museum Press, 2002.
JAMIESON, NEIL L. *Understanding Vietnam.* Berkeley, University of California Press, 1993.

QUANG PHÒNG. *Art in Vietnam: 1925–1945, The Fine Arts College of Indochina and Painting Before the Revolution; 1945–1954, Painters Volunteer to Fight for National Salvation; 1954–1995, From Socialist Realism to Postwar Multiform Tendency.* Hanoi: Association of Fine Arts, 1995.

RIDING, ALAN. "The Vietnam War, As Seen in Art From the Other Side," *The New York Times,* October 22, 2002.

THÁI BÁ VÂN. *Masters of Vietnamese Painting: Tô Ngọc Vân, Nguyễn Gia Trí, Nguyễn Sáng, Bùi Xuân Phái.* Hanoi, 1994.

VAN TAM. *War Sketches.* Ho Chi Minh City: Trường Đại học Mỹ thuật 2001.

WITNESS COLLECTION. *Phạm Thanh Tâm at the Battle of Điện Biên Phủ.* https://www.youtube.com/watch?v = 8kEbI89gqSs

Điện Biên Phủ and the First Indochina War, 1946–1954

ARGENLIEU, THIERRY D' (ADMIRAL). *Chroniques d'Indochine.* Albin Michel, 1985.

ASSELIN, PIERRE. "New Perspectives on Điện Biên Phủ," Explorations in Southeast Asian Studies, *Journal of the Southeast Asian Studies Student Association,* University of Hawaii Manoa, Vol 1 No 2, Fall 1997.

BODARD, LUCIEN. *La guerre d'Indochine: l'enlisement, l'humiliation, l'aventure.* Paris: Grasset, 1997.

The Quicksand War: Prelude to Vietnam. Faber, 1967.

BONNET, GABRIEL. *La guerre révolutionnaire du Vietnam.* Payot, Paris, 1969.

BOYLEN, KEVIN and OLIVIER, LUC. *Valley of the Shadow: The Siege of Dien Bien Phu.* Osprey Publishing, 2018.

BRANCION, HENRI DE (GENERAL). *Diên Biên Phu: Artilleurs dans la fournaise.* Presses de la Cité, 1993.

"Diên Biên Phu: le choc de deux artilleries," *Revue Historique des Armées,* 1992/4.

CHOMSKY, NOAM. *At War with Asia: Essays on Indochina.* AK Distribution, 2004.

CURREY, CECIL BARR and KEEGAN, JOHN. *Victory at Any Cost: The Genius of Viet Nam's Gen. Võ Nguyên Giáp.* Brassey's Inc., 1999.

DALLOZ, JACQUES. *The War in Indo-China, 1945–1954.* Rowman & Littlefield, 1990.

DUIKER, WILLIAM. *Ho Chi Minh: A Life.* New York: Hyperion, 2000.

FALL, BERNARD B. *Street Without Joy.* Harrisburg: Stackpole, 1961.

Hell in a Very Small Place: The Siege of Điện Biên Phủ. Philadelphia, 1966.

FOX, ROBERT. *Võ Nguyên Giáp.* Weidenfeld & Nicolson Military, 2005.

GRAS, YVES (GENERAL). *Histoire de la guerre d'Indochine.* Denoël, 1992.

GUILLAIN, ROBERT. *Diên Biên Phu: La fin des illusions.* Arléa, 2004.

HỒ CHÍ MINH. *Prison Diary.* Bantam Books, 1972.

Poems From the Prison Diary of Hồ Chí Minh. Small Press Distribution, 2004. ed. Bernard B. Fall.

On Revolution: Selected Writings, 1920–1969. Westview Press, 1984.

Patriotism and Proletarian Internationalism. University Press of the Pacific, 2003.

JOURNAUD, PIERRE. *Diên Biên Phu: la fin d'un monde*. Vendémiaire, 2019.

and TERTRAIS, HUGUES. *Paroles de Điện Biên Phủ: Les survivants témoignent.* Tallendier, 2021.

KARNOW, STANLEY. *Vietnam: A History*. Penguin Books, 1997.

LANGLAIS, PIERRE (GENERAL). *Diên Biên Phu*. France Empire, 1963.

LOCKHART, GREG. *Nation in Arms: The Origins of the People's Army of Vietnam*. Allen & Unwin, Sydney, Australia, 1989.

LOGEVALL, FREDERIK. *Embers of War: The Fall of Empire and the Making of America's Vietnam*. New York: Random House, 2012.

MARR, DAVID G. *Vietnam 1945: The Quest for Power*. Berkeley: University of California Press, 1995.

MORGAN, TED. *Valley of Death: The Tragedy at Điện Biên Phủ That Led America into the Vietnam War*. Random House, 2010.

NAVARRE, HENRI (GENERAL). *Agonie d'Indochine*. Plon, 1956.

PETERSEN, NEIL H. (ED.),

"Memorandum of the Meeting of the President's Special Committee on Indochina, Washington, January 29, 1951," *Foreign Relations of the United States, 1952–1954, Indochina, Vol. XIII, 1*. Department of State, Office of the Historian. S/S-NSC files, lot 63 D 351, NSC 5405 Series.

"Memorandum by the Chairman of the Joint Chiefs of Staff (Radford) to the President," in *Foreign Relations of the United States, 1952–1954, Indochina, Vol. XIII, 1*, March 24, 1954. https://history.state.gov/historicaldocuments/frus1952-54v13p1/d525

PIKE, JOHN. *Vietnam and the Cold War, 1945-1954: French Imperial Decline and Defeat at Dien Bien Phu*. Pen and Sword Military, 2024.

PRADOS, JOHN. *Operation Vulture: America's Dien Bien Phu*. DCA Kindle Edition, 2014.

ROUSSEAU, SABINE. *La colombe et le napalm: des chrétiens français contre les guerres d'Indochine et du Vietnam, 1945–1975*. Paris: CNRS, 2002.

ROY, JULES. *The Battle of Dienbienphu*. Carroll & Graf Publishers, 2002.

SAINTENY, J. *Histoire d'une paix manquée*. Fayard, 2ème éd., 1967.

SIMPSON, HOWARD R. *Dien Bien Phu: The Epic Battle America Forgot*. 2004.

STEWART, RICHARD W. *The US Army Campaigns of the Vietnam War: Deepening Involvement 1945–1965*. Washington DC: Center of Military History, US Army, 2012. https://history.army.mil/html/books/076/76-1/CMH_Pub_76-1.pdf

TASSIGNY, JEAN DE LATTRE DE (GENERAL). *La ferveur et le sacrifice, Indochine, 1951*. Plon, 1988.

TRUONG CHIN. *The August Revolution*. Hanoi: Foreign Languages Publishing, 1958.

Primer for Revolt. New York: Praeger, 1963.

VÕ NGUYÊN GIÁP (GENERAL).
> *Điện Biên Phủ: Rendezvous with History.* Lady Borton (transl.). Hanoi: Thế Giới, 2004.
> *Mémoires 1946–1954, Tome 2, Le chemin menant à Diên Biên Phu.* Paris: Anako, 2004.
> *Mémoires 1946–1954, Tome 3, Diên Biên Phu, le rendez-vous de l'histoire,* (translated by Huu Mai and Nguyên Van Su). Paris: Anako, 2004.
>> "The Most Difficult Decision," *Memoirs of War: Điện Biên Phủ.* Hanoi: Thế Giới, 2004.

WINDROW, MARTIN. *The Last Valley: Dien Bien Phu and the French Defeat in Vietnam.* London: Weidenfeld & Nicolson, 2004.

French Memoirs

AINLEY, HENRY. *In Order To Die.* London, 1954.

ANAPI (ASSOCIATION NATIONALE DES ANCIENS PRISONNIERS D'INDOCHINE). *Notre histoire.* Atlante, 2004.

BRUGE, ROGER. *Les Hommes de Diên Biên Phu.* Tempus, 2004.

DANG VAN VIET. *Highway 4: The Border Campaign (1947–1950).* Hanoi: Foreign Languages Publishing House, 1990.

EINAUDI, JEAN-LUC. *Viet-Nam ! La Guerre d'Indochine, 1945–1954.* Le Cherche-midi éditeur, 2001.

GALABRU, ANDRÉ. *La Victoire avortée.* André Galabru, Atlante, 2004.

GALARD, GENEVIÉVE DE, with BRAZIL, BÉATRICE. *Une femme à Diên Bên Phu.* Editions les Arènes, 2003.

GRAUWIN, PAUL. *J'étais médecin à Diên Biên Phu.* France-empire, 1956.

JOURNOUD, PIERRE and TETRAIS, HUGUES. *Paroles de Diên Biên Phu: Le Témoignage des survivants.* Tallandier, 2004.

LEONETTI, GUY ed. *Lettres de Diên Biên Phu.* Fayard, 2004.

LONG, PEDRO NGUYEN with WALTER, GEORGE. *La Montagne des Parfums, Une Saga Indochinoise.* Robert Laffont/Phébus, 1996.

PELISSIER, PIERRE. *Diên Biên Phu, 20 novembre 1953–7 mai 1954.* Perrin, 2004.

Additional Vietnamese Sources

ĐIỆN BIÊN PHỦ HISTORICAL VICTORY MUSEUM. "Artillery Regiment 351 in the Điện Biên Campaign." *The People's Army Newspaper Online,* April 23, 2024. https://rb.gy/2u0sv2

"Diên Bên Phu Campaign: 3 Fierce Attacks." *Government Electronic Newspaper,* May 2, 2024. *Chinhphu.vn.* https://shorturl.at/x7evb

VIETNAM MILITARY HISTORY INSTITUTE. *History of the Resistance War Against French Colonialism (1945–1954), Volume V.* Hanoi: People's Army Publishing House, 1992.

MINISTRY OF NATIONAL DEFENSE. Vietnam Military History Institute. *Winter-Spring Strategic Offensive 1953–1954: The Resistance War Ended Successfully. Volume VI.* Hanoi: Military Publishing House People's Team, 2016.

MINISTRY OF NATIONAL DEFENSE. Điện Biên Provincial Party Committee. *Điện Biên Phủ Victory: The Strength of Vietnam in the Hồ Chí Minh Era.* Hanoi: People's Army Publishing House, 2014.

NGO VAN CHIEU. *Journal d'un combattant Viêt-minh.* Le Seuil, 1955.

NGUYỄN HỮU ĐỒNG (Kỳ Thu). "Điện Biên Phủ Prisoners of War Are Grateful to Uncle Hồ's Soldiers." *Nhân Dân,* May 9, 2024. https://nhandan.vn/tu-binh-dien-bien-phu-biet-on-bo-doi-cu-ho-post808568.html

NGUYỄN TẤT LỘC. "Meeting the Former Artilleryman Again and the First Rounds of Bullets Fired at Him Lam to Open the Điện Biên Phủ Campaign." *baoxaydung.com.vn online.* March 26, 2014. https://rb.gy/9abjbb

NGUYỄN VĂN MAI. "Battle of Acupuncture Points in Đông Khê and Thất Khê." *The People's Army Newspaper Online,* November 6, 2011.

NGUYỄN VĂN QUYỀN (Colonel). "Civilians in the Điện Biên Phủ Campaign." *Institute of Military History,* April 26, 2024. https://rb.gy/4udop9

NHÂN DÂN. "April 3, 1954: Handing Over the Battlefield on the Eastern Slope of Hill A1 and Using Forces to Attack Base 105." *Nhân Dân Newspaper Online,* April 3, 2024. https://rb.gy/4go9zu

THANH HUONG. "French Prisoners of War at Điện Biên Phủ: Vietnam's Lenient Policy Has Awakened Us." *People's Army Newspaper, qdnd.vn online,* April 28, 2024. https://www.qdnd.vn/quoc-phong-an-ninh/chien-thang-dien-bien-phu-moc-son-lich-su/du-luan-quoc-te tu-binh-phap-o-dien-bien-phu-chinh-sach-khoan-hong-cua -viet-nam-da-thuc-tinh-chung-toi-773840

TRẦN LIÊN. "Điện Biên Phủ Campaign: Anti-aircraft Artillery and a Surprise Blow to the Enemy." *dantri.com.vn,* April 29, 2024.

VIETNAM MILITARY ENCYCLOPEDIA ONLINE EDITION. Volume 1: Military History. Hanoi: People's Army Publishing House. https://nvsk.vnanet.vn/chien-dich-thuong-lao-1954-29-1-13-2-1954-1-34308.vna

VIETNAM TELEVISION (VTV). "Điện Biên Phủ Victory and Numbers." *Việt Nam TV Online,* May 7, 2018. https://vtv.vn/trong-nuoc/chien-thang-dien-bien-phu-va-nhung-con-so-20180507183708329.htm

Editor's Acknowledgements

The new 2024 paperback edition of *Drawing Under Fire* is being published by Asia Ink in memory of the war correspondent and artist Phạm Thanh Tâm (1932–2019), who wrote his contemporaneous diary during his march from Yên Bái Province between February 21 and March 1954 and the fifty-five days of the Battle of Điện Biên Phủ.

After the English-language publication of *Drawing Under Fire* in 2005 by Asia Ink, and the French-language edition in 2011 by Armand Colin, I am thankful to Kim Đồng Publishing House for returning the diary to Vietnam, and publishing Phạm Thanh Tâm's original manuscript along with his drawings and sketches for the Seventieth Commemoration of the Victory of Điện Biên Phủ.

I would like to pay tribute to Phạm Thanh Tâm who, during one of the most sanguinary battles of the twentieth century that brought independence to Vietnam, retained his humanity and supported his comrades-in-arms through his art and writing in what US journalist Bernard Fall described as "hell in a very small place."

Mr Tâm gave me unrestricted access to his diaries and collection of war drawings between 2002 and 2015. Our frequent meetings took place at his house in Ho Chi Minh City and I would like to thank his wife Lê Thị Lân and his daughters Phạm Thị Thanh Hoa and Phạm Diệu Ly for their warm and unfailing hospitality throughout the project.

In Hanoi, my greatest thanks to Đặng Bích Hà and to the family of General Võ Nguyên Giáp (1911–2013). My gratitude to (bác sĩ) Nguyễn Thị Ngọc Toản, the widow of Cao Văn Khánh for sharing her memories of Điện Biên Phủ.

In Ho Chi Minh City, my special gratitude to Trần Thị Huỳnh Nga, the director of the Blue Space Contemporary Art Gallery, who introduced me to Mr Tâm. I was greatly helped by Nguyễn Toàn Thi (1946–2016), the director of the Ho Chi Minh City Fine Arts Museum, who gave me access to the museum's collection and archive.

My discovery of Vietnamese art created in war began when I first met Trần Thị Huỳnh Nga at an exhibition of the works of her husband, the artist Trần Trung Tín (1933–2008), at Gallery La Vong in Hong Kong. Trần Trung Tín in Ho Chi Minh City introduced me to the beauty and spiritual dimension of art created in war.

My thanks to the official war artists and performers who worked in propaganda during the French and American Wars (1946–1975), who shared their stories and art collections during my visits to Vietnam between 1995 and 2024.

In Ho Chi Minh City, I am grateful to Quách Phong, former director of the Fine Arts Association in Ho Chi Minh City, the artist Huỳnh Thị Kim Tiến, the actress Kim Chi, the lacquer artist Lê Quang Luan, and the war artist Nguyễn Văn Hoàng, former director of the Ho Chi Minh City Fine Arts University. In Hanoi, my thanks to the artists Trần Huy Oánh and Nguyễn Đức Thọ.

My knowledge of art under fire informed my decision to publish and edit *Drawing Under Fire* and was further shaped by my encounters with the war artists Huỳnh Phương Đông (1925–2015), deputy director of the Fine Arts Department of the Ministry of Culture and Information in Ho Chi Minh City (1977–1988), Lê Lam (1931–2022), recipient of the 2016 State Award for Literature and Arts, Nguyen Thanh Châu (1939–2012), war artist and director of the Fine Arts Association in Ho Chi Minh City, Thái Hà (1925–2016), a founding member of the Vietnam Fine Arts Association, and Thanh Ngọc (1920–2017), and Văn Đa (1928–2008) in Hanoi.

My gratitude to contemporary artists for their stories from the American Vietnam War: Nguyễn Đức Thọ, Nguyễn Thanh Bình, Lương Xuân Đoàn, and the sculptor Phùng Chí Thu.

In London, I would like to thank Jessica Harrison-Hall of the British Museum, the curator of the 2002 exhibition of Vietnamese war drawings at the British Museum, *Vietnam Behind the Lines: Images from the War, 1965–1975*, for contributing her wonderful preface and for sharing this adventure with me; and Robert Knox, Keeper of the Department of Oriental Antiquities at the British Museum from 1994 to 2006.

My thanks to Betty Yao and Katriana Hazell at Asia House with whom I co-curated *No More War,* the exhibition of works created during the Vietnam Wars by expressionist artist Trần Trung Tín, and by war artists Phạm Thanh Tâm and others.

My thanks to the Embassy of the Socialist Republic of Vietnam in London for their continued support, to ambassadors Vũ Quang Minh and Nguyễn Hoàng Long, and my special thanks to ambassador Trinh Duc Du, who hosted the launch of the first English edition of *Drawing Under Fire* at the London embassy in 2005.

My gratitude to Anandaroopa Nam Nguyen for his advice, support, and project management; and to the photographer Hans Kemp, who photographed Phạm Thanh Tâm's diary pages, drawings, and war memorabilia in the artist's collection and in the collection of the Ho Chi Minh City Fine Arts Museum.

My thanks to Nguyễn Vân Hà for her meticulous translation in 2005 and revision and notes in 2024, which benefited from newly available digitized Vietnamese archives and sources; and to Helen Cumberbatch for her assiduous and rigorous proof reading.

My thanks to the award-winning designer Misha Aniskt for his sensitive book design, inspired from his closeness to the subject from his father's letters written from the front at the Battle of Stalingrad.

My special thanks to my husband William Spurgin who shares my conviction that hope for an end to forever wars comes through understanding and respecting each other's histories. History that demonizes the "other" leads to endless war.